This book is dedicated to:

Jessica, Jamie, Penelope, Elessar,
and all those childlike souls
who delight in finding stones

Permissions

Contents

Contents

PART THREE
Stone Legacies: Stories from the Great Stone Sites

PART FOUR
Stone Power: Stories of Magic and Mystery

Contents

Acknowledgments

IN SOME WAYS WRITING A SECOND BOOK IS EASIER; in other ways, harder. I would like to thank all those who helped to make the journey lighter and less burdensome by sharing their wisdom, their encouragement, and their support. This includes my intrepid editor, Kate Epstein, my beloved family, my housemates, closest friends, and writer buddies—you know who you are.

I would especially like to thank three special men in my life: Bob Mann, for inviting me to listen to what stones have to say; Bill Grover, for tireless support in helping me with the detail work of producing this book; and Jim Crabtree, for his enduring love and unfailing faith in my work.

Finally, I would like to thank the stones themselves, for their guidance and enlightenment, for their willingness to be known, and for the connections they provide to a deeper, richer, more beautiful world. ☙

Introduction

You will find something more in woods than in books. Trees and stones will teach you that which you can never learn from masters.

—ST. BERNARD, EPISTLE

FOR MOST OF US, MOST OF THE TIME, STONES FORM an unassuming backdrop to the rest of our lives. They support the ground we walk on. They provide spectacular scenery for mountain hiking, climbing, skiing, or simply gazing. They help build the edifices that surround our lives: our homes, our workplaces, our churches, temples, mosques, and synagogues, our institutions of learning. Their very existence assures us that the foundation of things seems strong, solid, immovable, safe.

Yet stones have a far greater role to play. From our myths (my favorite is of the existentialist hero Sisyphus, condemned by the gods to roll a stone up the hill for eternity, only to watch it roll down again) to our legends (the search for the philosopher's stone, that Holy Grail of infinite prosperity) to oral traditions that speak of stone spirits, stones permeate our collective consciousness and the consciousness of Mother Earth.

Stones can teach us about our sacred connections— to spirit, to self, to memory, to imagination, to ancient energies, and to deep, archetypal urges. In the stories, poems, and meditations of this book, you'll find almost as many ways to learn from stones as there are stones themselves.

Standing before the great sacred stone sites and monuments—Stonehenge, Easter Island, Canyon de Chelly, the great Celtic standing stones, the temples of Egypt—creates a stir in our psyches like nothing else. You'll read how these ancient stones connected the authors to a transforming power that embodies the spiritual energy of the Earth itself.

You'll also see transformation in stories of the ordinary pebbles we feel compelled to pick up and slip into our pockets. Have you ever found a heart-shaped stone? A "holey" stone? A piece of quartz glinting on the ground, winking at you? Have you ever held a healing gemstone in your hand and felt a headache slip away, tension turn to ease, anxiety to calm? Then you know about the immense power that small stones have to bring their special teachings to us, and you recognize their truth.

Despite the seeming immutability of stones, there is also this truth: Nothing in this universe stays the same. Everything migrates with its own inner rhythm of change, of *coming from* and *going to*. Everything dances to its unique movement, however small and invisible it might be to the naked eye.

Perhaps it won't surprise you, then, to read tales of stones moving of their own accord—not over eons, but overnight. You'll find stories that describe the inner world of stones and others that describe thousand-ton stones moving themselves when called to do so. Mystery surrounds even something as "solid" as a rock.

You'll find more mystery in stories of rocks speaking: in a whisper, in a shout, in a musical lilt. They invite us to listen and to talk back—to sing, to cry, to speak what we hear in the deepest parts of our souls, in the echoed heartbeat of our longing for connection to everything in this world—especially to the wisdom of stones.

Finally, you'll read about memories created from encounters with stones. You'll read about rock-collecting relatives, grandmothers who planted magical stone gardens, and the arrowheads and grinding-stones of our Native American ancestors. The magical stones of childhood, the moments of transformation at sacred stone sites, the ecstasy of skipping stones, the discovery of secret stone refuges—these wonders await you. After reading these stone stories, you may never again pass by that strangely shaped river stone or that gleaming bit of quartz without pausing to look, listen, and reflect on the power and mystery of stone. ☯

Part One

Stepping Stones:
Stories of Healing and Empowerment

ETERNITY'S EGG
PATRICIA WELLINGHAM-JONES

Soft flesh wraps granite,
two perfect river stones—
in my hands the ovaries of time.

Another Version of Stone Soup

Maril Crabtree

ONE OF MY FAVORITE FOLKTALES IS THE STORY OF stone soup. Its origins are lost in time, going back several centuries, and attributed by various sources to Belgium, France, West Africa, eastern European countries, and others.

In one version, three hungry soldiers approach a village for food; in other versions a lone beggar, a monk, or a poor traveler asks for food. At house after house, the door slams shut with the same answer, "I don't have any food to give you."

At this point in the story, all versions agree. The hungry traveler's solution is to make stone soup by heating a stone in a large pot of water over a hot fire in a central location in the village. When villagers come along, one by one, and inquire about the unusual soup, its maker always responds that it would taste better if something more were added: potatoes, carrots, onions, tomatoes, a bit of meat. One by one, the villagers eagerly contribute the requested ingredients. Soon, the soup's delicious odor draws everyone to the simmering pot, and the villagers marvel at the taste of their own joint efforts.

One thing that makes the folktale so fascinating is that it seems to involve a bit of sly trickery. When no one gave a single bite of food, the traveler created the fictitious "stone soup" and enticed everyone to put something into the pot.

It's this aspect of the story that I find strange. Here's a wonderful story about overcoming greed, reluctance, fear, and isolation with generosity, cooperation, sharing, and making something from nothing. All these are positive values, but the whole enterprise starts with trickery and illusion!

Or does something else form the base for the lovely soup? Is stone soup simply an alternative way of looking at the world, a "think-outside-the-box" method that is so unusual it inspires others to do likewise? If you heard of someone making soup out of stones, wouldn't you be curious enough to contribute something when invited to do so?

When my publisher first suggested collecting stories and writing about "sacred stones," I was a bit like those grumpy, reluctant villagers who thought they had nothing to offer. I'd never been to famous stone sites like Stonehenge and Easter Island; I'd never had any miraculous healings from gemstones; I couldn't remember any mystical experiences in which stones spoke to me.

Then I took a closer look at some of my travels. I found enraptured journal entries describing my first trip to Arches National Monument or a trip to Greece, where I saw the ancient stones of the Acropolis and the Parthenon. I remembered a special rock beside a Colorado river where I often sat and mused, just because it felt so comforting. I found a poem I'd written about "talking stones" used in a Native American sweat lodge ceremony.

Bit by bit, my experiences with stones revealed themselves, and my stone soup got thicker and richer with each discovery. When I realized that I even felt a special relationship with my stone house, I knew I had simply ignored the obvious. "Sacred stones" are all around me, even when I'm not aware of their contribution to my life.

At that point, it was time to call on the universe to bring in even greater connections with stones. In that mysteriously wonderful way the universe has of responding to our hearts' desires, stone connections began to show up everywhere—in my life and in the lives of others. I used stones in my meditations and in my healing practice; I heard them speaking to me, offering their energy; I received stones as gifts. And the stories and poems that make up the savory soup of this book began to pour in.

In the beginning, maybe I had to "trick" myself a little into seeing stones in a sacred way, in the way I sometimes tricked myself into seeing my children as sweet angels, or my husband as the perfect lover. The rewards of such illusions in each case, it seems, brought me a sweeter life, an empowering interpretation of my world, and a richer "soup" to share with all. ◎

Poetry Stones
SuzAnne C. Cole

Poetry is a stone—
slate, granite, lava,
obsidian, marble, flint—
solid, imperishable,
each solitary stone
beautiful in its particularity.

Poetry is a stone
stubbornly blocking paths
stubbing toes
asking for acknowledgment.

Poetry is a stone skipped
across the water of reality
calling out—
Look here, look now, notice this.
Even in its sinking
ripples linger.

What parent, whose child
asks for bread,
gives instead a stone?
Bread is of the moment,
a stone forever.

One Smooth Stone

Ava Chambers

"Mommy!" Hanna yelled from outside. For a moment, her high-pitched three-year-old voice scared me.

"Look, Mommy!" she said, racing through the door and wrapping her arms around my legs.

Throwing the dishrag on the counter, I turned and grabbed her hands.

"What, baby? You don't have anything."

Grinning, she pointed as my father came panting through the kitchen door. His gnarled hands opened and revealed two pieces of driveway, three dirt clods, and one smooth, creek polished stone.

"We've found treasure," Daddy said, winking. Quickly putting their find into a napkin, he followed the bundle of energy that was his granddaughter as she went in search of crayons and paper.

I picked up the stone. I must have searched for millions just like it.

"Has Daddy taken every child he ever met on a rock hunt?" I asked my mother, who was making biscuits for our Christmas dinner.

Laughing, Mama said, "I suppose so. Rocks always were something special to your daddy. Remember the day you found out Daddy was a lapidary and you thought it was a bad word?"

As a child, I had almost pulled my neighbor's hair out for calling Daddy that. Lapidary, I found out, not only described Daddy's job but also his passion. He loved rocks, any kind of rocks. By day, he taught watch-repair and jewelry-making at the local technical college. Afternoons and weekends were spent searching the mountains of North Georgia for treasures. That search invariably included children of all ages.

Daddy tramped up Yonah Mountain and down through Nachoochee Valley, searching, teaching, and laughing. By day's end, he often looked like the Pied Piper as the leaf-lookers who invaded our mountains began to follow his lead and look to the earth for the power they yearned for. Almost all returned with at least one smooth stone in their pockets.

Now, age had robbed him of his agility. Years of pipe smoking left his breathing ragged and difficult. The only follower was my Hanna, the only treasure the one found in a fenced yard.

After lunch, my family settled down to open Christmas presents. Daddy smiled patiently as he opened neckties, winter gloves, and aftershave. Suddenly, he clapped his hands together.

"Look, look, a little pouch!" With a smile he asked my son, "Luke, did you make this?"

"Yes, Papa. I did it in Boy Scouts. I thought you could use it for your rocks."

"Papa," Hanna squealed. "You have a treasure pouch!"

"I sure do," Daddy answered. "Run to the kitchen and get our rocks."

"We made this for you," my oldest daughter said as she and her sister handed Daddy a huge card. Complete with glittered bells and feathered angel wings, the children's artwork brought tears to all our eyes.

Daddy solemnly folded Hanna's scribbled picture and put it inside his Christmas card. Placing the papers in the pouch first, he then added the stone, dirt clods, and gravel. Sitting back in his chair, he declared, "I do believe I got the best presents ever."

As twilight stole into the yard, we packed up the children and took one last picture. I felt a strange twinge of foreboding. Daddy raised his arm to wave good-bye. His little treasure pouch dangled from his fingers.

Mama stood blowing kisses. "Y'all be careful. Call us when you get home so we'll know you're safe," she said.

"I will. See ya! Love ya!" I yelled.

"Best Christmas ever," the children screamed.

What a difference a week makes. Daddy was gone just seven short days later. Remnants of a joyful Christmas were washed away with tears. Bits and pieces of joy rarely broke through our sorrow.

Six years passed, and my mother died. I felt overwhelming pain. The bitter pill of cleaning out my childhood home choked me. Friends helped me load furniture and take away the pieces of life that my parents had worked so hard for.

I sifted through drawers in the table that once sat beside Daddy's chair. Hanna pulled out a tattered pouch.

"What's this, Mama?"

My hand trembled as I reached for the best Christmas present ever.

"It was your granddaddy's."

Hanna opened the pouch, dumping the contents into her hand.

"Neat card," she muttered. "Who drew this scribble?"

"You did," I answered. Dirt and small bits of gravel fell between her fingers.

"This is a cool rock. Feel it, Mama."

I took the stone, felt its smoothness.

"This was Granddaddy's gift from you."

"What?" Hanna said.

"Daddy always carried a smooth stone in his pocket. He said rough stones were easy to find. But a smooth stone had been worked over by time. A smooth stone had been tested and tried, and ended up being pleasant to touch and to see."

Hanna turned a curious eye to me. "He saved it?"

"You found that stone with him the last Christmas he was alive." I said. "He had a gift from all his grandchildren that day. He saved what was the most valuable." Tears forming in my eyes threatened to turn to rivers.

"Was Granddaddy always searching for smooth stones?"

"Always," I answered. "He kept one to remind him that no matter how awful life could be, that . . ."

"What, Mama?"

I sighed. "I guess to remind him that he was always being polished. It reminded him that whatever trials he had to endure were merely polishing him, turning him into a thing of beauty. It kept him from giving up."

"It made him happy?" Hanna asked.

I nodded.

"Then, we'd better find you one." With that, she grabbed my hand and we headed outside.

I had been polished by the death of my parents. I suppose the loss of a few rough edges was more painful than I expected. Still, it was a new day, and there was a stone outside waiting for me to find, a smooth stone to put in my pocket. ◉

A Healing Gift
Will Davis

ONE DAY, I DROVE HOME FROM WORK, BUT AS I GOT out of my car, I began to feel dizzy. I thought perhaps I had moved too quickly, so I continued slowly into the house, holding onto doorframes and maneuvering myself into a chair where I could rest.

The dizziness continued, and as the evening wore on, it began to get worse. By 1:00 in the morning I was unable to stand or walk. The dizziness seemed the same whether I was standing, sitting, or lying down.

This condition persisted until about noon of the following day, when the dizziness finally stopped. I felt tired and unsettled. About three weeks later, a similar episode occurred. This episode lasted only a few minutes but was just as intense.

A few days later, while shaving, I looked in the mirror and noticed that the pupil of my right eye was much larger than the left eye. That really concerned me. I have worked in the medical field, and I know that only a few things could cause unequal pupils: a head injury, which I knew I had not had; a tumor; or a condition known as Adie's syndrome.

I went to see my doctor, but he could find nothing wrong. Neither could the ophthalmologist, but he confirmed that one pupil was noticeably larger than the other. There was no evidence of head trauma or tumor. The dizziness didn't return, though, and I decided to be grateful for that and ignore the difference in pupil size.

A few months later, in the course of my work as an artist, I met a woman who worked with healing stones.

"I have a gift for you," she said, handing me a small pouch.

Inside the pouch lay two polished oval-shaped pieces of malachite and a small, thin, clear quartz crystal. One of the pieces of malachite looked just like an eye, pupil and all.

"How interesting," I thought, remembering my eye problems and dizzy spells. I thanked her for the gift.

Not until I was working on one of my paintings a few days later did it strike me to lie down on my bed, close my eyes, and place the malachite stones on my eyelids. The stone that looked like an eye went over my right eye with the enlarged pupil. I placed the quartz crystal on my forehead between my eyebrows.

Next, I visualized my right eye becoming normal in size. I saw my entire head being bathed in an emerald colored light that penetrated through my head and into every fiber of my brain, blood vessels, neurons, everything.

Every day for five days I lay on my bed, covered my eyes and forehead with the stones, and repeated my visualizations.

After five days I stopped, feeling that whatever needed to be accomplished had been done. I have never had a problem since with dizziness or any other problem that could be considered brain related. My pupils are sometimes slightly unequal and sometimes normal, but they have never again gotten as noticeably unequal as they were. Although I have sometimes been skeptical about such things, I am convinced that the energy of those stones helped me.

A Healing Gift

Some time later, I met a woman at a function we were both attending. She complained of constant migraine headaches that seemed to build up behind her eyes. I told her my story and reached into my pocket for the little pouch of stones I still carried with me.

"Maybe these stones can help you the way they helped me," I said, giving them to her.

A year later, we saw each other again at the same function.

"I did what you told me to do, and I haven't had a migraine since," she told me.

I hugged her and said, "I'm happy for you. Maybe you can pass on the stones to someone else who needs them."

I don't know if that happened, as I have not seen her since. But I hope that somewhere out there, someone who really needs the power of those stones will have received them from someone. If you ever see two malachite stones, and one looks just like an eye, perhaps you received those very stones! ☺

All Stones Are Broken Stones

Karen Lee Lewis

All sounds
    move

Stones receive this
  — music —

slow
time
  broken

    into
      pieces

Stones compose us.

Note: The poem's title is a line from the poem
"Vectors," by James Richardson.

Oracle

Susan Kerr Shawn

MIDMORNING. THE DIRT ROAD ALONG THE CHAMA River hunkered down under simmering dust, fragrant with sagebrush and pine. I was on the lookout for rattlers, a rock, and the rest of my life.

Late the night before, I listened to coyote's timeless call bounce back and forth across the narrow canyon mesas, lacing the darkness snug along the riverbed below. I'm a rain-forest woman, an Oregonian, so desert wilderness sounds keep me alert.

On a week's silent retreat at a Benedictine monastery deep in Georgia O'Keefe's beloved land, I lay on the sleeping shelf in my tiny adobe cell. It was so quiet that other people's thoughts in that canyon floated into my mind like dreams.

During the gentle shift from night to dawn, I decided to call a rock to me. I wanted to listen to it speak of my work in the world. Many threads were coming together in my life, but the pattern wasn't yet clear. The colors were still dark, changing shape like smoke. I'd been in city government for over ten years; then, through a beloved's death, my work evolved into the healing profession, which was once again in flux. What is my life's work *now*?

The next morning, about two miles down the road from the monastery guesthouses, my rock found me. Toward the quietly chattering river on my right, about twenty feet from the dusty road, it called my name.

"Over here. The big one that's resting all alone. What about me?"

Around the size of my outstretched hand, it glowed. I leaned down, picked it up, and held it in my arms, feeling with my fingers where the river had soothed it, seeing stone stories swirling through it. It weighed about four and a half pounds, just about right.

Sweat mizzling down my neck, I carried my rock first on one hip and then the other, back and forth, down the road to my room. After noon prayer and silent lunch with the monks, I walked back to my cell, smudged with sage, anointed the rock with massage oil, and prayed. Hard.

Years ago a vigorous shaman taught me to commune with rocks, to see deeply into their wisdom. Rocks are silent beings everywhere in our midst, holding our stories on a geologic scale, the earth's Library of Congress.

Asking my question again and again, waiting to see what appears in response, I simply list up to four images I receive from the top, the bottom, and each side of a divination rock. An abundance of twenty-four images is possible. It's a little like the game we play when we're kids, to name what we see in the clouds overhead as they eddy and change form.

I then condense these images from the rock and knead them by prayer and intuition into a recognizable answer. It's part soul projection and part rock, dancing together in synchronicity and mystery, flying on a thread of faith that everything truly is alive. Even rocks.

I sat on the earthen floor staring at my rock, and it stared back at me, blind.

"What is my life's work, now?" I leaned forward, cursing myself silently for thinking answers lay in a rock. I sat. And sat.

Slowly, someone or something flipped the "on" switch, and the rock lit from within. Before my eyes a slide show began, one picture forming as the last dissolved: *A crone looking west, severe, sharp-eyed under a cowl. Two hands, doing bodywork. A priest on fire, serene, looking east, comforting someone. Myself, emerging from a threshold, carrying a book of light.*

Holding my journal in my lap, my pen skipped along trying to keep up with this show. Outside, wind rattled the door as the afternoon rain hurtled into overflowing arroyos. Turning the rock to another side, I watched intently as it continued:

A heart on fire, with a woman of light emerging, assisted by a dark figure with antlers. Two huge hands holding a tiny baby whose head is catching light on its crown from the east. A dark butterfly, wings outstretched, heading toward the light, and the light racing to greet the butterfly. A woman in prayer on a mountain, surrounded by golden light, swirling. A wolf watching a rainbow.

One side had four images overlaid like transparent, peeling wallpaper: *a muzzled dog, over a sleeping lamb, over an evil demon, over a creature of light that was part human, part angelic.* On another: *A person on hands and knees peers through a hole to the lighted realm.* Fourteen different animals showed up: *wolf, owl, eagle, bear, butterfly, dog,* and so on.

This was all on the video channel, so to speak. On the auditory channel, I heard only two words "Editor. Writer."

After each side had shown me its pictures, the One who runs this show tenderly shut the light off, and we rested, smelling the desert after the storm. Outside a rainbow blazed.

Grateful, I gathered up the threads of my answer: *deep knowing, smiling, watching alertly, doing bodywork, heading toward the light, holding head in grief, talking and arguing, comforting someone, emerging, peering into the lighted realm, carrying a book.*

I carried my rock home in my lap on the plane to Oregon. It's here with me now, alive with desert oranges and brick red veins, and its mysterious deep inner light. Sometimes I worry about keeping it so far from its home, but it speaks to me still, so I guess it's okay. It lives on my altar below a handpainted Green Tara thangka from Tibet.

Today, I offer bodywork, body-centered psychotherapy, and a wild brand of spiritual direction, all woven together as in my rock. And I am beginning to write that book I saw. Ho! ☉

Penumbra   Phyllis Becker

I feel as cold and hard
as it must feel on the moon.
No warmth, even on the light side.
And what, my dear, is hidden
in the dark, right beyond
the separating line? We say we will
always tell the truth. So many lies
hidden there—yours and mine.
We hold hands and I will the plants
to grow and a way out of all the lies
that did not seem like lies,
only to be revealed like the moon:
darkness cupping light. And the world
is still spinning and I'm dizzy.
Where are you? I read our old letters.
They seem silly now. My shoulders
droop, my eyes are bloodshot.
The moon doesn't move.
How do we move beyond it all?
Is it a leap of faith, finding our way
in the dark, or facing a harsh bright light?
A friend said she had to leave town
before her heart turned to stone.
Another nurses her grudges as tenderly
as she never was. I want to count
my lucky stars but don't count much
on anything, just keep track of the
weather, its colors, feel, and smell.
Keep an eye on that loony old moon,
that crater-pocked piece of rock
nestled in velvety black.

Crystal Power

Joy Cummings

WHEN MY IMMUNE SYSTEM STARTED TO FAIL, I did not trust modern medicine to heal me. Intuitively, I instead sought answers from the spiritual realm.

For a long time I had yearned to have a deep spiritual life, to meditate, to listen to the quiet voice within, but I did not have the faith to trust that inner voice. I had been raised to believe that the mind was the only true guide; emotions, feelings, and "intuition" were not dependable.

As I searched for healing and spiritual truth, I wanted to trust that voice. I wanted to understand the mysteries of the universe. I wanted the ultimate wisdom, and I wanted it immediately. I did not comprehend that patience is part of wisdom. I had never been drawn to crystals and was not even sure I believed in their power, but I had read how they were used in sacred ceremonies. Some years before, a girl had come into my clothing store, selling handmade crystal earrings. When I declined to purchase any, she gave me one of her pieces, saying it would change my life.

Because my ears weren't pierced, I hung my new crystal on the wall behind the counter. My ailing body eventually forced me to close the store, and the crystal was either sold or given away. But later, as my spiritual search deepened, I wondered if a crystal just might contain healing power.

Since my youth, I had been attracted to Native American culture and had read numerous books. My studies began to take on a more than academic interest. I found that I was adapting the spiritual beliefs of native people.

I attended powwows in the area, drawn by the pulsating drums and the scent of burning sage. This combination spoke to me and quieted my soul. Before leaving a powwow one day, as I browsed the retail booths set up around the grounds, I passed a table of crystals and other stones spread out for sale. I thought of buying one, but an inner voice urged me to wait.

Soon after the powwow, I climbed a hill on my daily walk. In spite of my illness I still found the strength to hike in the nearby hills. The earth, plants, sun, and wild creatures seemed to give me the energy I needed to get through the day.

As I followed a dusty road along the plateau, a stone caught my eye. I bent down to pick it up and noticed another one nearby. Examining them in the sun, I realized the first stone was a fragment that had been broken from a small geode, with tiny, almost microscopic crystals crowded inside its outer crust. My heart fluttered as I gazed at the crystals. How had they come to be in this obscure place? I did not know. They were not the large prisms I had seen at the powwow, but they were still crystals and they had been provided.

The other stone was a chunk of pink quartz—not the clear pink crystal of the rose quartz, but the milky, rusty pink of the local quartz. I sensed that the pink of the familiar local stone was just as powerful as the transparent radiance of the rose quartz, a universal symbol of love. I knew the stones were a promise that I would not only be healed, I would also find the spiritual answers I was seeking.

Eventually I did heal. I have learned many secrets of the universe, but I now know that they can never be learned all at once. I know that this learning is a lifelong experience.

Today, my stones sit in a beautiful hand-thrown clay bowl on my bathroom counter. They nourish me each morning as I prepare for the day. ☺

The Power of Pipestone
Robert M. "Bob" Anderson, Ph.D.

RECENTLY, I ACCEPTED THE POSITION OF COMMAND chief master sergeant for the 147th Fighter Wing of the United States Air Force. This honor exceeded my expectations and was, at the time, the high point of my military career.

In the 1970s, the air force's chief master sergeants adopted the American Indian chief as their symbol. The induction certificate states that "The United States Air Force today only promotes one percent of its enlisted force to the rank of chief master sergeant. Today's chief must be a teacher and mentor, and is looked on for leadership of the enlisted force."

I grew up in the politically incorrect days when kids used to play cowboys and Indians. Crazy Horse of the Cheyenne, Chief Joseph of the Nez Perce, and Sequoia of the Cherokee fascinated me. My grandmother, Alma DeShazer Anderson, was French and Indian, a native of Tennessee. She had been born in the late 1800s and was not registered on any Cherokee rolls. We are part of the tribe that is now called "the lost ones."

To me, making chief was not only a great honor; it was also a calling to reconnect with my Native American heritage. One day a wonderful thought came to me: "I need to make a peace pipe." Native Americans know the peace pipe by many names, such as *coup pipe* and *calumet*. Some just called it "the Pipe." Many tribes used antler, soapstone, or even wood to make the bowl, but the traditional pipe was made of a certain red stone known as pipestone.

True pipestone comes from a quarry near the appropriately named town of Pipestone, Minnesota. It is a reddish rock that, when quarried, is soft and easily worked with hand tools, even a knife. When exposed to air, it hardens. The tribes that use this rock consider it sacred. Some believe that the red of this rock is the blood of their ancestors. The making of a pipe, using only hand tools, is a significant sacred event.

I obtained a block of pipestone from Minnesota and traced a traditional design. With a set of files and a coping saw, I set out to fashion my pipe. I roughed out the shape of the bowl and the base. I cut holes for the bowl and stem.

Then I let the stone tell me what was inside it. I sat with the bowl and shaped it with the files. Slowly a set of wings appeared around the front of the base of the bowl. Next came a star (a star appears on the rank chevron of the command chief master sergeant), and finally a diamond (which indicates the rank of first sergeant on the chevron).

I filed, sanded, and polished the bowl for close to 400 hours before I was satisfied, and then I started working on the stem. Unable to find any local sumac, the traditional material (except for the poisonous kind), I went through several frustrating attempts at drilling a hole through a pin oak branch. Finally, I succeeded. After tying several feathers and carving designs in the stem, I assembled the pipe. Pipe and stem successfully connected on the first try.

With its soft red color and white star occlusions, the pipe looks like a miniature constellation that dropped from the sky and turned to stone. This stone has a sacred power of its own; it connects with people, even those with no Native American heritage. I saved the dust created by the filing and sawing and gave it to several friends in small glass vials. I told them it was magic dust, and I sense that there is, indeed, magic in this stone. I felt a great sense of serenity and peace while I worked on the pipe. Nothing I have ever worked on with my hands filled me with such a sense of accomplishment and purpose. ☯

Stones David Ray

At times you see the world as it was—
a scene ventured into by pioneers
or even the dinosaurs well before them

or some of the people in between,
a passing scenario, just a glimpse
of how earth was with more forest, less

of what we've brought. Not so much granite
had been converted to gravestones.
Some sea creatures had not yet become

limestone. Even one hard shard of flint
was sometimes enough for survival or rescue.
We, of course, grew up scorning stones,

had no holy pebble to caress for good luck,
nor was hope for immortality assured by a jewel.
But even in a dream to see the world as it was

before sabers and cannons and too much fear
and too many words is a great joy, most often
achieved at dawn before gentle pink clouds conspire

to lure us back to the age of dread, the rule of
the ubiquitous giant mushroom and the men
who worship it, at the edge of the stone age to be.

Strange indeed that men renounce fiery dawn for that.

Rune Walk

Shirley Fritchoff

THERE IS A PLACE ON THE SEA OF CORTEZ WHERE magic dwells—a vortex of energy where the desert meets the sea. Waves pulse in from the south, and mountains landlock the beach to the north, east, and west. In season, the pelicans migrate in numbers that darken the sky. Schools of small fish shadow the water, as dense as seaweed. The great birds circle and plummet to dine exceedingly well.

Here I discovered the magic of stones swept up from the depths. Over millennia, under tremendous pressure, the womb of the sea has forged these small matrixes into forms alive with imagery and symbols.

My first awareness of runes came from *The Book of Runes* by Ralph Blum. The book arrived with a pouch containing twenty-five small clay tablets, each imprinted with a rune symbol. The instructions directed the drawing of a tablet (rune) from the pouch and looking up its meaning in the text. The message was always relevant, even uncanny. This was an authentic voice I could trust.

I felt a relationship between the small, beautiful stones I found on the beach and the ancient Viking runes. Blum suggested developing one's own set of runes, and to this end I collected twenty-five smooth stones from the sand. With a felt pen, meticulously, I copied the rune symbols on each stone. It was an exercise in totally "not right." I could feel the protest. When I tried to clean off the offending ink, it was impossible. Humbly I took the stones back to the beach and scattered them into the sea.

I still felt urged to make my own runes—finally, not to make them but to find them. The search began. Finding the arrow of the Warrior came quickly, as well as Partnership, an "X." Three more came along, but it was apparent I would never find all twenty-five. Another wrong track.

I gave up collecting and etching, but the feeling persisted: The key was out there, awaiting discovery. Now and then a stone would stand out from the rest. I'd study its uniqueness but usually drop it back to the sand. The essential link was missing.

I continued to be drawn to these unique stones but didn't make the connection that they might be a different kind of rune. My breakthrough came from a most unexpected source.

A friend who lived another 200 miles further into Mexico used to stop at my place for an "overnight" as she drove to or from Tucson. Her stopovers could stretch into days. A devotee of an Eastern guru, she trusted in her master to see that my hospitality was always there for her and that there would be food she could eat in my refrigerator. But my kitchen wasn't vegetarian "kosher," and her judgments were unending. I couldn't hope to be valid until I knelt at the lotus feet of her guru. A day or two of this I could handle, but the judgments and criticisms became too much. I felt used and finally said no.

If this was Buddhism, spare me.

The morning after she left, I was walking on the beach, muttering to myself, but, as always, scanning the sand for treasures, when right in my path a perfect little Buddha looked up at me. It drew me like a magnet—his round face, two little eyes, fat belly, and flowing robes. I held the stone in my hand, shocked out of my mutterings. "When the student is ready, the teacher comes."

I knew a teacher had come. This teacher brought me the key to the rune stones. I carried my treasure home. With it cradled in my left hand, I filled journal pages with feelings and questions. It was my morning of discovery. It was all right to say no and to recognize that ten trips to India doesn't anoint one with Buddha consciousness. I'd thrown the baby out with the bath water.

This was my first experience of being taught by a stone. The key to unlocking the mystery of these Runes from the Sea had come at last. I was learning to listen with my heart.

What makes a stone (or anything else) a rune? You do. There is no set of rules. How do you read a rune? With your feelings. Give rise to your intuition and memory. Listen with your third ear and with your heart. When there is true yearning for meaning, it will come.

Take an imaginary rune walk down the beach. Practice awareness and being present. Walk in the rhythm of your breath. A stone catches your eye. Bend down to look closer. Does it draw you? Pick it up, and look at it with your full attention. How does it feel? What do you see as you gently turn it in your gaze? Be aware of your feelings as the image emerges into focus. Don't try to analyze, just feel. Your feelings will tell you whether you hold a rune or a rock. (The same stone can be a rune for one and a meaningless rock for another.)

The difference between viewing a Rorschach inkblot and a rune stone is that now the ball is in your court, not an analyst's or therapist's. Sometimes you may get the message at once, but this is rare. Few runes are Buddhas. You'll need some special tools: an attitude of trust, your journal, and private, unhurried time and patience to give your rune.

"To draw a thing is to become." When you sketch what you see, one image may lead to another. It is a rare rune that limits itself to just one figure or image. Look for opposites. If you see one well-defined eye, chances are you'll discover the other. Write your feeling response to your drawing. Let the figures lead you. Trust. A cardinal rule of journal writing is honesty. Please don't try to control a rune voice. Runes are like dreams. If you already knew, you wouldn't need the dream (or rune) to lead you.

I chose a rune stone with a very clear image for an exercise with a group. The stone was passed around the circle of seven women, silently, and each wrote down what she saw. I had expected some variance but not what came. The seven totally different responses ranged from "an old man leaning on a cane," to "a vagina with a penis," "storms," and "a rose." Not one saw the unmistakable clown that led me to choose that stone for the exercise.

We live in a society of instant gratification. Read the misleading titles on the self-help bookshelves. "You can have it all, and you can have it now!" Inner growth doesn't come prepackaged like a roll of cookie dough you can slice and pop in the oven for a delicious treat in just seven minutes. Growth is a process. It is like a seedling that can take a lifetime to bear fruit.

There are many teachers on the path. Some are quite unexpected, and others we are slow to recognize, like critical houseguests and runes. Nature's runes are all around us. Practice seeing and listening, cultivate awareness, and listen to your feelings—your guides into the secret world of hidden treasures. ◯

The Warming Stone

Patricia Walkenhorst

THE LITTLE STONE STILL HELD MY FRIEND'S WARMTH as she took my hand and placed it deep in my palm. When my fingers closed over the hard surface, it felt like the stone had been formed there, instead of being tossed smooth in surf and sand half a world away. On it was written, "To share with a friend is to see twice the beauty."

When my husband's company transferred our family to another city, my neighbor, Pat, gave me the stone as a symbol of our friendship and a reminder of the close bond we shared.

In the course of packing and moving, I lost track of the stone.

We had been settled in our new house only a few months when a hovering blanket of loneliness engulfed me. I longed to visit Pat, to share again the fun of decorating our homes, our love of flowers. Life in the new city was fine, but it lacked the consolation of having a trusted friend nearby.

One bone-chilling midmorning after the children had gone to school, freezing rain clattered against our windows, and a thick glaze of ice soon covered the streets. Radio news warned of a severe ice storm. I was homebound and completely alone, with no family or friends to talk to, disheartened and discouraged in this faraway suburb of preoccupied, self-sufficient people. The storm soon cut off the electricity and downed the phone lines.

I felt like a prisoner in my own home. I decided to shake off my growing despair by balancing the checkbook. Busy work. When I pulled open the desk drawer, out tumbled the little stone. It was ice-cold. But when I laid it in my palm, as Pat had done a few months before, it warmed me as I warmed it, and I smiled. Later that day, I wrote a letter to her, telling her how the little stone she gave me nudged me enough to help me cope.

Company transfers took us to other cities, and our family learned to savor the adventure. When the children married and my husband retired, we moved to the South to enjoy a leisurely life on a golf course. Most of our neighbors were healthy and active, but one man brought his wife, Mary Lou, to the resort to spend her final days in that peaceful environment. Her brain cancer advanced slowly and took years to claim her life. She had wonderful care and was comfortable, but she was oblivious to life around her.

When I visited her, I felt a kinship—a friendship, though I didn't know if she knew me or even that I was there. I talked to her about the yellow pollen falling from the pine trees outside her window, the flowering dogwood near the glistening pond, and the abundance of pink camellias this year; all of them seemed to grow in beauty as I spoke.

During her last days, I longed to do something for Mary Lou. I knew I would miss her. Rummaging through the desk drawer one day, the little stone again tumbled into my hand. It was cold when I picked it up, but I pressed it between my palms and it became warm. I walked with the stone in my hand to Mary Lou's house and asked to see her.

Only a sheet covered her. She was beautiful, her body feverish in its fight for life. I placed the little stone deep in her palm, and she closed her fingers tight around it. It stayed clenched there for days, until the spirit left her tired body.

When she died, Mary Lou's husband brought the stone back to me. It was still warm—warm from Mary Lou's hand to his, from his hand to mine, as it had been from Pat's hand to mine, and mine to Mary Lou's. Over thousands of miles, over troubled times and good, it conveyed friendship and caring from one human being to another. The writing on the stone was fading, so I traced over the letters: "To share with a friend is to see twice the beauty." ◯

The Pebble Clock

William Keener

We gather round the basket
every month, and one of us,
without a word, reaches in,
lifts out a little stone. Cool
and smooth its weight lies
in his hand. He takes this
gift to carry in his pocket,
leave atop a distant peak,
or set on temple steps,

his to place upon a grave,
or throw into the sea. One
man chooses for all eight,
one rock a month to mark
the bond of friends. Given
time, only one will survive
to hold the final stone.

The basket we have filled
with wave-worn pebbles
is our slow impassive clock,
an hour-glass to measure
lives. Instead of sand, out
go pebbles, reminding us
that every thing we love
tick, tock, rocks away.

Zen and the Art of Stone Skipping

Mary-Lane Kamberg

THE MORNING OF THE GREEN ROCK SKIPPING Contest of 2003, Tim Burelle was at work. Walking outside, he spotted a stone on the ground. Something about it made it stand out from the others.

"There's the winning rock," he told his boss. He picked it up and put it in his back pocket.

The contest he planned to enter was part of the annual Spinach Festival in Lenexa, Kansas. It was the third year in a row that Burelle would compete. The previous two years, he had fallen short of his goal of winning the rock-skipping championship. This year, he hoped, would be different.

Stone-skipping experts say that choosing the perfect pebble is an art in itself. "A rock that's just right for someone else won't be right for you," says Mickey Hamilton, who has won the green rock skipping championship thirteen times since 1989. He is the sole inductee in Lenexa's Green Rock Skipping Hall of Fame.

"Make the letter C with your thumb and index finger," he says. "Then look for a rock to fit—one that feels good in your hand and on the tips of your fingers, so when you throw it, you can get a little extra spin on it. The rock should be about two inches in diameter and as smooth as possible, so rough edges won't catch the water's surface and stop the skip."

Along with choosing the right rock, participants need a bit of technique. But, as Hamilton says, "Nobody teaches you how to skip a rock. You just do it as a kid. You can either do it or you can't."

Contestants in the Green Rock Skipping Contest each get three throws, and a three-judge panel decides the winner based on number of skips in each contestant's best toss. In order to forestall endless debates, the number of winning skips is not announced—getting an accurate count is difficult. The rocks skip so fast, they're hard to see. In fact, verification of any attempt to set a Guinness World Record requires videotape that can be replayed in slow motion. Without such equipment, Green Rock contest judges rely only on their powers of observation.

The contest is just for fun, but for Burelle, stone-skipping is also a spiritual, Zen-like thing. "You have to be one with the rock, one with the release, and one with the water," he says.

Burelle is not alone in his spiritual approach. According to the Web site for the North American Stone Skipping Association (NASSA) in Driftwood, Texas, "NASSA believes that stone-skipping is a uniquely ancient activity that touches something very special in those participating."

Stone-skipping dates back at least to ancient Greece. Another word for it is "dap." In England, the pastime is known as "ducks and drakes." In France, it's *ricochet*. In Ireland it's "stone skiffing," and in Denmark it's *smutting*. Hindi, Russian, and Chinese languages all have words for it. No matter what the act of stone-skipping is called, it seems to be enjoyed around the world by people simply standing on the edge of a creek, as well as those competing in official contests.

During the 2003 Green Rock Skipping Contest, Burelle was down to his last throw when he slipped the lucky rock out of his back pocket. He tossed it over the 1.5-acre pond known as Rose's Lake. He watched it skip approximately 150 feet to the opposite shore. But in rock skipping, it's the number of skips—not the distance traveled—that matters. Judges counted about sixteen skips—far fewer than the current Guinness World Record of thirty-eight skips established by Jerdone Coleman-McGhee in 1994 on the Blanco River in Texas, but more than the dozen or so skips recorded for Hamilton, who placed second.

And Burelle's interest was in the title, not the world record.

"I'm about three feet off the ground!" he said, clutching his first-prize ribbon. "It's been a three-year battle trying to dethrone Mickey."

And what about the splash of Zen?

"When I let the rock go," Burelle said, "I knew it was the winner." ◯

A Lantern in the Dark

George Arbeitman

I BOUGHT IT AT A TRADE SHOW. IT WAS NOT SHINY OR polished or even pretty. It was coarse with deep grooves, vaguely triangular. Yet I was drawn to it.

When I wear it as a pendent, it grounds me. It has a warm energy that enters the heart and radiates out. It's like a cup of hot soup in winter or a cozy, warm blanket on a cold night. When I wear it, I often feel a shift in awareness, a deeper sense of focus and purpose.

This translucent olive-green gemstone, called moldavite, comes from the hot core of a huge meteorite that fell to earth some 15 million years ago. It landed in the Moldau valley of Czechoslovakia, the country my mom comes from. I feel a powerful connection with her when I wear the stone. Often, images of Mom come to me when I'm wearing the moldavite, images from our younger days, a different era: a Brooklyn tenement filled with cooking smells, stuffed cabbage, baked fish, sometimes a treat like chocolate pudding, where I get to lick the spoon (and the pot!).

After the meal, if she was in the mood, Mom would tell stories of Europe, of how she wanted to come to America despite her father's forbidding it. With great courage and determination, she came anyway, alone, twenty-two years old, on a six-week boat trip surrounded by strangers.

While she was on the boat, the news broke of war in Europe. The hounds of hell and holocaust decimated

Europe and devoured Mom's family, leaving her with a haunted heart. Her only legacy was survivor's guilt, which was served liberally in soups and salads or spread on toast with jam.

As a child, I was a sponge, soaking up her smoky malaise, smothered by shadowy dread. I withdrew. My only refuge was the fantasy land of storybooks. There were nightmares of monsters in the closet, of drowning.

Now moldavite is my lantern in midnight dark, a shining light that guides me on a journey into my inner realm. Together, we open up closed doors. We find dark, dusty corners where ghosts sleep, and gently we call their names. We invite them to arise from slumber and voice their wounds. Thus the heart may be healed. Ancient grief can be laid to rest. Together, we can befriend the most savage childhood beasts, perhaps transform them into loyal friends.

Moldavite has a gentle intensity, urging me to open up, to risk. When I wear it, I feel buoyant, as if resting on thick clouds. Often I experience tiny streams of light, a shower of particles that usually center in my stomach as vibrant heat.

Sometimes while wearing my pendant, an insight, fully formed, will come to me. Other times, as I relax and stretch out, a series of images comes. Here is one that had deep impact. I see a sad-faced gloomy-eyed young boy—me. My parents are shouting. Thrown dishes smash against the kitchen wall as a quiet truce shatters into deadly splinters. "Why do they fight?" "What did I do?" "It's me, my fault!" "I'm bad." "No peace, no peace, it hurts!" Another boy appears, with shining eyes and a shy smile. He looks like the sad boy's twin, my twin. We embrace. For an instant, our parents are there. We also embrace, and they leave. Two adults appear. One is sullen, moody, the other relaxed, warm. All are parts of myself.

We are in a circle, hands joined. We share our pain, our joy. A yellow light flashes through us, forming a glowing, spinning thread that weaves again the fabric of our lives. We swing into and through each other's space, separating, merging, becoming one another, completing a sacred cycle. Darkness and light coalesce, two sides of the same coin.

It is a fall day. I decide to try a new way home. It is twilight, and the sun is slowly melting into shadow. The quiet streets are unfamiliar. I remind myself that it's okay. My vision softens. In the distance, green trees intertwine with winding back roads and glinting sunlight to create a serene collage.

In the stillness, the whispering wind sighs. I have not worn my stone for awhile. I like to take breaks until it feels right. Tonight, before sleep, I will put it on. I just might have luminous, healing dreams. ☺

The Red Stone
Tonweya

IN THE SEVENTIES, MY HIGH SCHOOL TOOK A LIBERAL approach to teaching, with far-ranging courses on philosophy and world religions. Teachers were allowed to dress however they wanted and to be who they were. My journey with the red stone first began when my philosophy teacher invited several of us students to her home. When we arrived, the sweet, amber odor of incense drifted in the air. Strung beads covered the doorways. Soft music played in the background. Her home felt full of peaceful energy, as if you were soaking in a hot tub on a cold winter's day.

My teacher asked us to sit on the floor and came back with a sack of rocks. She laid them carefully on the floor.

"I'd like you to spend some time with these stones," she said. "Look at them, touch them, feel them. See if there's one stone that calls out your name."

I looked at the stones and noticed the colors, shapes, and sizes. I felt swirling energy coming from them, surrounding me. I felt like the Milky Way embraced me. I picked the stones up, one by one, noticing that some had circles in them. Some had faces, and some had lines that curved and twisted like the river, twisting and turning until it flows into the ocean.

"Now," she said, "choose a stone that you would like to keep."

I held many stones in my hand, but one captured my eye. It was orange, yet you could see the blending of dark red in it. The red stood out to me. There was a distinct translucent line that formed a circle around the stone. It reminded me of life, and I thought of how we exist in a great, infinite circle, endings intertwined with beginnings.

I held my red stone for a long time, feeling the fire inside it. That fire was the blood that rushed through my heart. I did not know its full meaning, yet I knew there was something special about this stone.

Since that time, I have collected stones of all types, receiving them as gifts from the earth. Each stone reminds me of the time in my life when I found it, but each also tells its own story of the mysteries of the universe. Some are considered holy rocks, others crystals, and others still have no names attached to them.

I have learned what stones represent in different cultures. I have studied what the colors can represent, ways to tell whether the stone has female or male energy, and how stones were used in healing the human body. What stands out for me is that stones contain life's wonderful energy. This awareness has led me to my soul's conviction: that all of the earth is sacred. All is related. I am the stone and the stone is me, and we are both of the same world.

Many years have gone by. The red stone has remained with me. It moved wherever I moved. When my life was out of balance, I held that red stone in my hands. When moving from one place to another, you exist between two worlds, the one you are leaving and the one you are entering, and a transition takes place.

During those times, I often felt out of balance, out of harmony. I turned to what would help me ground. Since the red stone represented new beginnings to me,

I took it out and held it to remind myself that this ending was really just a beginning.

When I held the stone, I heard its messages. Sometimes I was told to ride the wave, let my life flow like the river even if its waters became rapids and crashed down on the rocks below them, for the rapids would cleanse me. Whatever was holding me down, I could rise again refreshed. It was like standing out in the rain, letting it lightly fall on my face, allowing the waters to renew me.

There were also times when the red stone simply appeared in my life. When I went through hard times, or during one of my frequent moves, the stone presented itself to me so that I could see it.

I would question it. "Why are you appearing in my life now?" I realized that not only did the red stone directly convey information to me, it also became a conduit, allowing messages to appear. Often after seeing the stone, I came across something that gave me encouragement to go on or to follow the path that was intended for me.

Sometimes the world became a dark place for me, like a shade being drawn down a window. At such times the red stone reminded me that I, too, was a part of the whole, and that I, too, was sacred. The red stone's healing message soothed me, and my spirit could thrive once again.

Stones are also record keepers of times and deep knowledge. Many years later, I discovered one of the main reasons that the red stone entered my life.

My totem is the red-tailed hawk. The fire of the tail is the fire of the red stone. The bands in the feathers are the striations in the red stone. Hawk is a messenger, reflecting childhood visions and dreams and pointing the way to a place where they can be empowered and fulfilled.

Hawk usually comes as a totem at a point in life when you are beginning to move toward your soul's purpose. The bird is a catalyst for transformation. The beautiful red stone, also a messenger and a catalyst, prepared the way for Hawk. ☺

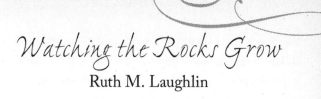

Watching the Rocks Grow

Ruth M. Laughlin

For Yvonne Nordstrum Levenson,
my audacious Tucson friend

I painted my house with a very small brush.
You laughed, certain I'd give up. I used my grinder,
put two coats over the undercoat. I worked all
summer. That year I took back my maiden name.

Like the fish story in reverse, each time you told
the story, the brush got smaller. You relished telling
how incredulous you were that I persisted. It was
a meditation for a divorced sculptor teaching
in an old-time Mormon town.

Either you went to bars, people said,
or you went to church. We chose Bill's Bar for both.
I watched local cowboys watch you play pool,
witnessed their admiration and awe.
You were audacious, leggy, a Tucson-grown woman,
long curly mop of hair combed back with fingers.
Your saucy tone pierced the dim-lit, male climate,
incensed with chainsaw shavings and cigarette smoke.
Particles of haze floated through the air,
supplications offered from burning tobacco
suspended in the raftered sanctuary.

A banker in town told me all I could do on my
budget was to sit and watch the grass grow.

(continued on next page)

There wasn't much grass in high desert country.
When it rained, water flowed through my front yard,
a flat stream. Among the junipers, scrub oak, and
ponderosa, nothing but washed-over dirt stayed.

It took some years and uncountable trips to
streambeds to hunt for chunks of petrified wood
and rocks of the right shape and color. I planted them
in curves in the front yard, beginning with the fire pit,
and under the trees to the road.
I sat on the porch and watched them spread.

I wonder, did you ever go back? Before
I left the White Mountains, I planted bluebells,
buttercups, Indian paintbrush, larkspur, marigold,
and owl clover around and through the rocks. Years
later, on my return, those rocks—framed and punctuated
with wildflowers—
had turned the barren dirt into a work of art.

Crystal Children

Phylameana lila Désy

STONES THAT MAKE THEIR WAY INTO OUR LIVES ARE similar to newborn babies.

Like a new baby, each new stone brings its unique energies into our space. These various energies challenge us to explore the places within our lives that require expansion. A particular stone may challenge your viewpoint. Another stone might expand your horizons, while yet another could stretch your creativity, and so on. Ultimately, one way or another, all gemstones can help to promote personal growth in each of us.

When the purpose or lesson that a stone offers has been realized, the stone will often move along to another place or into the hands of another person. You may discover that you have misplaced a favorite stone that had become a good friend, or you will feel an urgency to give a particular stone to another person. This is the way of stones. They belong to no one forever. Although we may feel sad when we lose a cherished stone, it is natural for stones to leave us when the appropriate time has come.

This is also true of our children. We are their caretakers only for a few short years. At some point, if we have done our parental jobs well, children will grow wings and venture out on their own. Each child will develop at his or her own speed when making strides out into the world.

I have been enormously blessed in motherhood. I gave birth to three beautiful children, two sons and a daughter. The years when they were under my care to nurture and love have become precious to me. I still have close relationships with my children, but our relationships are continuously evolving. Their needs are very different now from when they were very small.

A few years ago, while vacationing in the Caribbean, I took a nature walk along a worn pathway near the beach. Low in the bushes, I spied a small bird's nest. The nest was empty, and I instinctively knew that it was waiting for me. This small, now-abandoned nest symbolized for me my own struggles with my empty nest. I gently picked it up, wrapped it in some tissues, and tucked it carefully inside my beach bag to carry home with me.

That nest was not meant to be empty for long. Soon afterward, I came to possess three egg-shaped gemstones that I have since gently placed inside its hollow. I feel that the stones are in small ways representative of the children who no longer depend on my constant care. The largest blue stone is a chrysocolla, the medium-sized stone an orange calcite, and the smallest egg a black-and-white speckled stone known as snowflake obsidian. The energies and properties in each of these stones are as varied and unique as the characteristics and personalities of my three children.

Some days, when my head is filled with thoughts of my children, I hold these three child-stones for a few minutes, cupped in the palms of my hands. On other occasions, I pick up and clutch closely in my hand only one of the stones and hold it alone, as my mind wanders in the direction of one son or my daughter.

Feeling the stones' warmth and vibration energies in my hands reminds me of how I am forever energetically connected to my children, regardless of distance.

Perhaps, one day, I'll have grandchildren to love and pamper. If I do, it would not surprise me if more egg-shaped "grandchild-stones," representing the unique essences of these children yet to come, find their way to me. They will take up residence in that little nest I saved from the island, keeping good company with the three child-stones I now cherish so much in my not-so-empty nest. ☺

Matthew's Rocks

Penelope Holder

THE BEACHES OF SOUTHWESTERN ENGLAND ARE mostly large pebbles, perfectly smooth and worn by the sea, which brings them in and takes them back out with the tide. As a child, I loved to scramble over the pebbles with my playmates to see who could go the fastest without slipping and falling.

Some of the beaches, though, are pure white sand glittered with spray from the waves. On these beaches Matthew Perkins, my brother's oldest child, loved to run. He excelled at running, just as he excelled at everything else in life.

Matthew was fascinated by the rock formations in different parts of his homeland, and he loved pointing out to visitors the centuries-old rock walls and cobblestone streets still seen in English villages. His fascination with rocks evolved into a passion for climbing mountains—what are mountains, anyway, but large rocks?

When Matthew left college, he traveled the world teaching English to underprivileged children. In his spare time, he climbed whatever hill or mountain he could find in the area. For Matthew, the harder and rockier the climb, the better.

With his father and his younger brother, he climbed Mount Snowdon, in Wales. Matthew scampered like a mountain goat while the other two struggled. When they reached the top of the high peak at last, they saw Matthew waiting, sitting on a rock.

"Isn't this super? The air . . . it's so clean!" he said, while the two others gasped for breath.

After a brief pause, he was off, running down the mountain. The other two took one look at each other and decided to take the train back and wait for him in the car park. Matthew, amazingly, beat them to the car. There he stood, holding a small red rock that looked as though it should have come from the Grand Canyon.

That rock accompanied him on his travels, together with a compulsion to climb every mountain he saw. He collected rocks from every country, in every formation and color he could find, and when he returned to England between trips, he labeled each rock: where he found it, from what mountain, and in what year.

He visited the United States, where I live, and Canada, where my sister lives. In my home state of Georgia, he climbed Brasstown Bald as well as Stone Mountain about eight times, collecting rocks from each one.

Roughly six months after his return to England, my brother called and told us that Matthew had Hodgkin's disease. He underwent radiation, chemotherapy, and steroid treatments. After a year and a half, he was in remission. This time he chose to stay in England, but that didn't stop him from climbing Mount Snowdon again, over and over.

Unfortunately, the cancer returned, and Matthew couldn't outrun or outclimb the vicious disease. Doctors tried, unsuccessfully, to find a suitable bone-marrow donor; as a last resort, they did a stem cell transplant. He spent months in and out of hospitals.

By this time, everyone knew his love for rocks of all kinds—crystals, quartz, uncut gem stones. They showered him with stones, gifts that might bring some comfort when he could do nothing more than gaze out the hospital window and remember his climbing adventures.

In his last year of treatment, Matthew wanted to climb Helvellyn in the Lake District, England, a mountain more treacherous than Snowdon. His mother was reluctant, but his father said he would go with him, and promised they would be all right.

As his father reached the top of the mountain, he became worried. He had lost sight of Matthew. Then he saw him, placidly sitting on a rock.

"This time, Dad, I honestly thought you would be waiting for me," he said.

Matthew died on August 24, 2003, at age twenty-eight. When my sister and I arrived in England, we stayed in his flat and packed up his belongings. We came across his rock collection, all labeled, in perfect condition. Some rocks sat on the windowsill; some were wrapped in tissue. In all, we counted forty-seven different kinds of pebbles, rocks, and crystals. I was not surprised. He loved the earth and hated what was happening to it, but no one could crush his beloved mountains.

At the funeral, my sister and I each held one of his rocks in our hands. My rock was from India, the land of my birth. Matthew would have liked that. This story is my tribute to him. Now he can climb mountains higher than any he ever climbed and run as fast as he wants. ☯

Memorials

Regina Murray Brault

Slabs of blasted granite
ride chained to flat-bed trucks
announcing sunrise
as they rumble to stone sheds
where men with Old World names
chisel cherub wings and epitaphs
then tour cemeteries with their children
to view these unsigned works of art.

The poems that wake me in the night
come like pebbles
thrown against a windowpane.
They are uncut and rough
full of flaws and fissures
but they're mine
to chisel, polish, sculpt
into angel wings and epitaphs
that bear my signature.

The Simon Stone

Valorie J. Wells

I STOOD IN THE MEDITATION GARDEN AT THE entrance to the Stations of the Cross Prayer Walk. The sun was barely visible, a slender line of pale yellow in a robin's egg blue sky. My chest was so tight I could hardly breathe, even though the early August dawn was cool. The nightmare that had started when I was only twelve years old was actually coming true: Mom was dying. Today. I had nothing left in my bag of tricks to keep her here on earth, with me, forever. And I had to admit that, at eighty years of age, she had surely fought the good fight against heart and kidney disease.

Mom had optimistically endured three years of dialysis for kidney failure and now, at last, she had deliberately succumbed to the inevitable: gangrene in both feet. My whole life had been sucked down into a murky fog of disbelief ever since the day at the hospital when Mom calmly offered her decision to the surgeon. My closest sister, Gail, and I listened in shock as Mom smiled, her Irish eyes sparkling, and said, "Well, I think that I would like to go to Heaven with both my feet so I can dance on the clouds. So, Doctor, I think we should stop the dialysis and will you please cancel the amputation for me?"

The nuns in the assisted living center had given our family a lovely three-bedroom apartment on the first floor, and we had permission to visit with Mom at any time of day. We had been warned that her kidneys would not last more than ten days. I made the dreaded telephone calls to my other two sisters who lived far away. Through tear-choked words, I managed to tell them the situation.

"Mom is valiantly waiting as long as is humanly possible before taking morphine for the pain, but I don't know how much longer she can hold off," I told them urgently.

When my sisters arrived from the airport, I slipped out of the room to give them time alone for Mom's blessing. She had been holding court as the queen of the assisted living center, her beloved Pomeranian, Peter, at her bedside. With that incredibly brave and benevolent smile and in a whispering voice wracked with pain, she shared happy memories of each person's contribution to her peacefulness, from the janitors to the hospice nurses and cooks.

Now I walked along the center's manicured garden paths, but I had no idea where I was headed. The only sound I could hear was the faint song of wind chimes on a patio nearby. My eyes were drenched in tears.

"This is it. Mom is really dying, and it's quite clear that today is the day," I mumbled to myself.

In a zombie-like shuffle, I entered into my nearly forgotten childhood routine of "saying the stations": genuflect, make the sign of the cross, meditate on that portion of the last walk Jesus took up Calvary, and say the prerequisite prayers. This time-tested Catholic ritual of meditation and devotion was as comforting and familiar as slipping on a pair of old sandals. I felt my spirit unwind and say, "Ahhhhh." By the time I had reached the fifth station—Simon of Cyrene Helps Jesus Carry the Cross—I was weeping.

I sank to my knees and cried aloud, "Oh God, I can't weather this storm alone. Where is my Simon to help me carry this cross?"

When I opened my eyes, I saw a rather large, dull black stone resting atop the stone path at my feet. The brick walkway was trimmed neatly, edged with low and tight boxwood hedges. At the foot of each of the wooden stands, intricately carved with the scenes of Jesus' last walk on Earth, lay a base of rounded river rocks. Just a pile of plain, ordinary, round-edged rocks holding up this panorama of holy significance. And yet, there was this one stone at the edge of my sandal. It seemed to whisper, "Come on, turn me over and see what you'll find, Valorie."

The underside of this common stone sparkled with a surprise of silver flecks and a pink ribbon of rock that sparkled in the early morning light. For some reason, I felt better simply holding it in my hand. I finished my prayers with a deep sense of calm. Just a silly stone, but it seemed to convey a quiet peacefulness and hope. This stone was a reminder to expect surprises and hold out hope. I slipped it into my skirt pocket as I finished my prayers and meditated on the divine order of our birth-to-death journey. Somehow, I felt calmer each time I rubbed my thumb and forefinger over it. Just a simple stone. A Simon Stone.

When I went back into Mom's room, I was pleased to see that all three of my beautiful daughters were there. The midmorning sunshine sparkled through the window on Mom's face, turning her skin translucent, as her rasping breath reminded us that this was not an ordinary visit with Grandma Wells.

It was three-year-old Kyrsten who broke the tension. My little granddaughters, Kyrsten and Emelie, were playing on the floor all around Mom's bed. We tried to keep them quiet, telling them to not disturb Grandma's rest. In typical toddler style, Kyrsten reached into my skirt pocket and found my Simon Stone. She gently removed the rock and smiled at me for approval. I nodded "Yes," thinking, what harm can a simple stone do now? In seconds, the clever child discovered the clanking sound of rock on metal.

Twang, twang, twang, went the Simon Stone on the metal frame of Grandma Wells' deathbed, as Kyrsten and Emelie clapped and giggled with this ancient music. All at once, Mom turned to me and offered a weak smile and a nod at the joyous clamor.

"You will be the grandma now," she whispered. Speaking without words, she shared her vision with me, in one of those cosmic moments that happen in a flash of time and space. The next Christmas Eve family buffet would be at my house. Mom was ready to let go of her place of honor. She had passed the Matriarchy Mantle to me now.

Every woman in the room held her breath, from the sovereign of our clan, to the nurse nuns, to Mom's menopausal daughters, right on down to my youngest daughter, the expectant mother. We all froze in that moment of ancient connectedness: women who bond with music, laughter, and the sheer joy of children. The Simon Stone had served its purpose, and I accepted my rightful position as the head of the family.

The nuns began to softly singsong the rosary. As Mom mouthed the words in unison, she smiled one last time and went to dance in the clouds. ☾

An Infinite Stone Healing

John R. Ellis

MY JOB HAS BEEN EXTREMELY STRESSFUL FOR THE last two years. When I started having a feeling of heavy pressure on my chest and had a hard time breathing, I went to my family doctor. She ordered a stress test that showed some problems in my left ventricle and referred me to a cardiologist.

Two days later, before my appointment with the cardiologist, the chest pressure got worse. I felt pain down my left arm and drove to the emergency room. After nitroglycerin pills, blood thinners, and morphine proved ineffective, they admitted me to the hospital.

The next morning the doctors ordered an echocardiogram, which also showed something blocking my left ventricle. They scheduled me for a heart catheterization and an angioplasty, or bypass, depending upon what they might find. Although I was scheduled to have the procedures done that morning, several emergencies kept me waiting all day. I was in constant pain.

While I waited for the operation, my friend Marilyn came to the hospital with a variety of healing tools, including two Infinite stones that her husband, Bill, had bought just a week before at a local shop. Infinite, the shop's owner told him, was a recent discovery from South Africa, a combination of serpentine and chrysolite, with remarkable healing properties.

"Bill told me he had a headache that day. He had already taken aspirin, but it had no effect," Marilyn said.

"After he walked around the store for fifteen minutes with one Infinite stone in each hand, his headache disappeared."

She handed me the stones as she began an energy healing treatment. She also placed a piece of black tourmaline first at my feet, then on my chest above my heart.

Thirty minutes later I was taken back for a second echocardiogram. Results appeared the same: a blockage in the left ventricle. Back in my room, as I awaited surgery, I held the Infinite stones for another half hour, then fell asleep. When I awoke, I noticed that the pain had lessened.

About an hour later, I was wheeled into the operating room for the catheterization procedure. The operation lasted only twenty minutes. The doctors couldn't find any blockages or other problems with my heart! They were at a complete loss to explain why two echocardiograms had shown significant blockages.

Many people were praying for me. I truly feel this was a miracle healing from the Creator with a giant assist from the Infinite stones, black tourmaline, and my dear friend Marilyn. Bill gave me the two stones, since it was obvious to him that they were meant for me.

As an added note, I work around concrete a great deal and have developed a severe skin condition because of the acidity in concrete. Over the years I've tried several prescription medications to help heal this problem, to no avail. After coming home from the hospital, I put one of the Infinite stones on my hands every evening. In just two weeks, the skin problem was totally cured.

Months later, I am still feeling fit and well. But I've learned my lesson. I've decided to quit my stressful job and become a massage therapist. ◌

Meditation

RECEIVING A STONE HEALING

Gemstones and other stones can be powerful sources of healing, as some of the stories in this book attest. Massage therapists sometimes use smooth, heated stones to enhance their work; special training is available to learn techniques with stones. Energy healers may use gemstones to enhance both the release of energy blocks and the infusion of energy to achieve a greater level of well being.

Stone healings can range from the placement of a single gemstone directly over an energy center to the creation of elaborate patterns with many gemstones surrounding the entire body. Sometimes healers hold a specific stone in the hand, rather than placing it on the body.

If you are considering receiving a stone healing, check with reliable sources to find someone reputable and qualified. In addition, use your own intuition, guidance, and discernment. Stone energy is not for everyone. Try this meditation below if you are uncertain:

1. In a quiet place, preferably outdoors, close your eyes and relax. If possible, sit on the ground. Ask the universe to make its wisdom available to you. After clearing your mind of other thoughts, declare your intention to seek an answer to the question: "Is this the time for me to experience stone energy through receiving a stone healing or massage?"

2. As you sit in a relaxed state asking this question, observe what images, thoughts, sounds, and smells come through on your inner mind screen. Wait until you sense that you have received what you need. It may be a word, a phrase, a picture, or a sound. It may simply be a feeling that you can identify. Some of you will receive your answer through this process; others may go to Step 3.

3. Open your eyes and look around you with deliberation, mindful of the question and intention. What is the first thing you see? If there is a stone within view or within reach, pick it up and hold it. Notice any messages you receive, including how you feel. If you don't see any stones, wander a bit to see if any turn up. Sometimes this activity in itself produces an answer; if there's an absence of stone where stone might usually be, perhaps the answer is "no."

4. If it's impossible to be outdoors, try this meditation indoors. Gather a symbol of each of the four elements (earth, air, fire, water). For example, use a feather for air, a candle for fire, a stone for earth, and a bowl of water for water. Place yourself in a circle with the symbols around you. With eyes closed, turn and extend your hand over each element. Notice any sensations, messages, or images that come with each. If you sense positive images with the earth element, this may guide your decision.

Part Two

Stone Memories:
Stories of Recollection and Remembrance

BEACHBOUND
CRIS STAUBACH

fooling in the depths of quartz,
contemplating moons of Jupiter
as the tide sinks away,
my grandmother stoops
among small stones,
mesmerized.

A Century of Stone
Maril Crabtree

THE JAYS' INSISTENT CAWING INTERRUPTS THE silence of my stone haven. Birds don't respect the sacred mood silence brings. As I sit on the deck, a robin lands in front of me, a huge worm wriggling in its mouth, the rapturous prospect of dinner making it oblivious to my presence. A few seconds later, off it flies, leaving the usual gift on my white-streaked rail.

Hearthaven is the name of my century-old stone house. A haven with a heart. An invisible heart, yet one that clearly beats to its own rhythm, as anyone who has lived in an old house can tell you. This house's rhythm is slow and stately, dignified and delicate, like the huge wings of a monarch butterfly folding in and out, or the breathing of an old woman as she sits in her favorite chair staring into her memories.

A broad porch spreads like a welcoming bosom across its yellowed limestone front, supporting arched pillars. Boxes of red geraniums adorn the stone steps. A cluster of ribbons and vines smiles from the middle of the front door—a door as old as the house, solid oak, scuffed and scarred with the comings and goings of generations of occupants.

Who were those occupants? I know nothing of Hearthaven's first owners, although I suppose they were a family sizable enough to fill most of the six bedrooms. One psychic overnight guest sensed the friendly ghost-spirits of two children, standing by the rocking chair in the corner of her bedroom. She described them as two young girls dressed in old-fashioned "Sunday best" frocks with large hair bows and sausage curls. Were they visiting their former playroom?

In the fifties and sixties, the social phenomenon known as "white flight" emptied the neighborhood. The stone house, like others, stood vacant while market values sank lower and lower. Finally, a realtor bought it and cut up its majestic interior into tiny apartments.

Years of neglect and indifference followed. I picture the house sagging into a state of mourning for the ignominy of its condition: the fine, old wood cracked and dry, the mortar between its aging stones crumbling, dust invading its bones. Neighborhood lore has it that violence swept through its rooms when one tenant, in the midst of a domestic quarrel, shot and killed his wife, then killed himself. The house stood vacant once more.

Finally, a large family with more vision than pocketbook bought the house as a bargain in a "bad" neighborhood and restored it. They tore down the makeshift apartment walls, replastered the rooms, and installed new wiring and plumbing. The splendid oak woodwork framing hallways and staircases emerged from its painted disguise. More years flowed by. The house withstood the rambunctious patter of six pairs of young feet with little damage other than a banister rail or two kicked loose.

And still the house waited for me. The family that restored it moved to a more upscale neighborhood, one with better schools and lower crime rates. My stone sanctuary sprawled, exhausted but welcoming, in the middle of the block, a "for sale" sign once again propped in a corner of the yard.

It was love at first sight. The rugged stone walls reached out and wrapped me in decades of gentle hospitality. I bought it the first day it went on the market, sparing it the indignity of standing alone again for months or years like so many of its companions.

Now this magnificent stone house and I will age together. I'm glad it has a few decades' head start. Someday I'll be too tired to climb the stairs to my third-floor study. I'll move my writing desk into the dining room, where I can look out lace-curtained windows to watch starlings, jays, and mourning doves flit through the silver maple trees. When I'm too tired for the second-floor climb, I'll doze on the big green living room sofa, comforted by solid stone walls.

In those later years, the house and I will share the sacred stone silence of early morning hours, when only we old ones are stirring. I'll sweep her stone steps and savor the fresh smell of dewy grass while I watch the sun's progress across the porch columns. The bird droppings on the deck rails won't disturb the house's measured stone breathing. After all, birds and other living creatures have a prior claim on earthly space.

It's satisfying to speculate that this century-old haven may outlive me, may still be creaking and breathing through its limestone lungs long after I'm in the ground somewhere nearby. Maybe I'll revisit it then, as a bird streaking across the deck, or a butterfly folding its wings in and out, with solemn dignity. Or maybe I'll meet the ghost-children. We'll visit the playroom together, surrounded by the comfort of stone. ◠

Stone Houses

Terry Forde

These stones, stolen from the rivers,
are the bookmark of centuries.
They have slept in the footprints
of mastodons and their lichen blankets
took a hundred years to weave.
They have known the caress of ancient oak roots
and seen fish begin to walk upon the land.

Now we imprison them in mortar,
no longer bathed in the cool of glaciers.
Gone is the kiss of a salmon tail
and a bluebottle's wing on their cheek.
They have been torn from their brothers
after a million years of family.

They are locked in straight lines,
their faces in the wind,
dust covering their dreams.
But deep inside, fires still glow,
for these stones know that one day
they will be given back to the river
when we are all gone.

Rocks and Restoration

Kathleen Craft Boehmig

I SLOWLY GOT OUT OF THE CAR AT THE END OF A discouraging day. The gray February sky matched my mood as I retrieved the mail. Weeds grew around the mailbox instead of the pansies that had languished in flats for several months before my husband finally tossed them into the compost heap. I looked at the neglected flowerbeds in our yard. Busy with other pursuits, I hadn't planted any spring bulbs, mulched around the Japanese maple, or cut back the English ivy, which threatened to choke out everything in its path.

I reached down to move a large rock that had been kicked into the middle of a raised flowerbed. It resembled a petrified gray Irish potato. I smoothed the dirt off its dimpled surface, and then I recognized it. It had belonged to my grandma, Essie May Brown, and had come from one of the rock borders she fashioned around her flowerbeds. Holding that rock took me right back to the 1950s, to Grandma's garden on West Shadowlawn Avenue.

"Why do you have *so* many flowers, Grandma?" I wiped the perspiration from my forehead, getting dirt on my face. At age four, I wasn't worried about a little dirt.

"Flowers are my life," she said. "When I sit on the sewin' room floor hemmin' up a dress for one of those party debs I sew for, I think about bein' out here in my garden, with all of God's beautiful flowers . . . and with you, my Sweet Man."

"I'm not a man, Grandma. I'm a girl," I grumbled, but I grinned up at her. She always called me that. Nobody in the family knew why she chose to call me her Sweet Man, but I didn't really mind. I spent a lot of time at Grandma's house while Mom accompanied Dad on his business trips, and Grandma and I were the closest of buddies. Grandma made everything seem like an adventure, from picking up pins in the sewing room to planting bulbs, as we did that day.

"Don't drop this'n on his head," she warned. "Dig him a little hole here—oh, that's a good'n. Now put him right there, not too deep, and point his little head up so he can poke it out to the sun. Okay, let's give him some water, he's *thirsty*. Give him a right smart more so he can start to grow. That's enough. He says thank you, ma'am!"

Most all of Grandma's bulbs grew lavishly into the sunlight. In the spring, her backyard was a gardener's dream. First the white, yellow, and purple crocuses unfurled their heads from spiky leaves. Then came the snowdrops, dainty snowflakes, exotic sherbet-colored daffodils and narcissi, outrageously garish Dutch tulips, and yellow clouds of forsythia.

Easter time brought a snowstorm of pink and white dogwood blossoms, with lacy white, pink, and lavender hyacinths underneath. In summer, hydrangea bushes reared their blue and lavender mopheads, with fragrant climbing roses in the background.

A charming white picket fence surrounded it all, like a frame around a lovely picture. In the very center of the garden rose a giant old pecan tree full of chattering squirrels and birds, a beautiful raised flowerbed at its base. A rock-border necklace encircled the garden with old-fashioned pansies. It was truly a paradise for a little girl who learned many of life's important lessons digging bulbs with her grandma.

I held a rock from that border now, forty-three years later. I had taken it from Grandma's garden when the house was sold after her death. The new owners mowed everything down, tore out the picket fence, and installed a chain-link enclosure for their Doberman. Only the old pecan tree and memories remain.

Well, I thought, that's not really all that's left. Grandma's favorite gifts to us were, of course, flowers. My mom, aunt, and uncle have her flowers growing in their gardens, and Grandma gave me a Woburn Abbey rosebush that out-blooms everything on our street.

I gently placed the old rock at the edge of my flowerbed and pulled up a weed. I noticed something green under an overgrown holly. I pushed aside some pine straw and recognized the grasslike spikes: five mounds of Grandma's Star of Bethlehem!

The tears came as I grabbed a trowel and gardening gloves, and gently weeded around these symbols of my heritage. Just then the sun broke through the clouds and shone down on Grandma's flowers, still thriving in this weedy patch of earth. My grouchiness dissipated as I restored the flowerbed, and my five-year-old son ran to hug me. "Whatcha doin', Mom?" he asked.

"See those little plants, Sweet Man?" I said, brushing dirt off my son's sweaty face. "Sit down here with me, and I'll tell you all about them." ◯

Generations of Stones

Jeanne Ann Ryan

I HAVE LOVED STONES AS LONG AS I CAN REMEMBER. My grandfather, a geologist, gave me the gift of loving pretty rocks, crystals, stones, and minerals when I was a child. Grandpa Keith was a door-to-door encyclopedia salesman during the Great Depression. As he roamed the country selling his books, he plied his trade as a geologist. He studied the strata of the land, wrote grand theses about faults in the earth, and collected fossils and rocks of all kinds. These beautiful pieces remain in my garden and home.

When we were young, Grandpa gathered me up with my brother and cousins for weekend field trips. We learned to love rocks for their color, their beauty, their feel, and their energy.

These field trips, Grandpa's legacy, had a profound effect on our lives. We all chose scientific fields of study. I chose biology. My brother chose aerodynamic engineering. One cousin became a nurse. My other cousin, a struggling C-student in college, raised his grade average enough to stay in college because of the A he earned in geology.

This love of stones stayed with me as I became a healer. Certain stones, crystals, and just plain rocks called out to me. They wanted a place in my home. They wanted to take part in my healing practice.

I use crystals and stones to amplify healing procedures. Stones vibrate at different frequencies, and they can be used at certain body points where that frequency is needed. The decision about which stone to use is often intuitive. I go inside my sacred space and ask which stone will enhance the healing. As the healing progresses, I keep the awareness of that stone or crystal integrated with the energy of the healing. The stones can help healer and client reach depths that were previously unavailable.

Certain stones and crystals are good for clearing your home or office. My favorite is an eight-inch-long six-sided double terminated quartz crystal. When I use this crystal for clearing, I circle the room, beginning in the east, and sweep the disharmonic energy into the crystal with mental focus and intention. I then hold up the crystal point and mentally release that energy to its Creator source, to be used only for unconditional love.

A small amethyst wand, a tall rose quartz pillar, a large rutilated quartz, and a round rose quartz eye are among my other favorite stones. The large piece of phallus-shaped rutilated quartz was my father's personal stone, given to him by Grandpa. Dad considered it a cross between a good luck piece and a health aid. He cherished that stone, but he kept it on a shelf behind his desk. When I asked why it was hidden, he admitted that Mom wouldn't let him display it because of its shape. Dad gave me the stone before he died. He was right; it is a powerful healing stone, and I enjoy thinking about him when I use it.

My grandchildren tease me about being "the rock Grandma." But I love all of my rocks and stones, and I have noticed that my grandchildren are developing that love also. Some of my prettiest stones disappear into suitcases as the grandchildren return home. That is as it should be. ☺

The Thinking Stone

Suella Walsh

I CAN'T REMEMBER A TIME IN MY CHILDHOOD WHEN the stone wasn't there. It stood proudly in the northwest corner of my grandmother's yard, standing nearly four feet tall with a width to match. It had a grayish hue.

When I was a preschooler, relatives often placed me on the stone when they talked to me. Doing so put us more at eye level. Even at that age, I was drawn to the warm vibes that enveloped me while I perched on the cool, smooth surface. Even more importantly, the stone made me taller, empowering me by lifting me up.

When I was big enough to climb onto its welcoming expanse, it became my special place—my place to think. Since I was an introspective child, this rock afforded me the perfect environment to contemplate, to analyze, and to make important life decisions. The stone also became a symbol of my dear Irish grandmother. She was a true light in my life—someone who encouraged me and believed in me.

It was a natural progression that by the time I was old enough to sit on the stone (without having to climb up) it became the place where I spent many circumspect hours. I felt safe there, wrapped in the serenity of the stone, feeling wrapped in the cocoon of my grandmother's love.

On clear spring or summer days, when the sun warmed my back and the sky was so blue I could see right through it, I sat on my polished gray throne and contemplated life's choices with all their shades of gray, all their subtle innuendo. Ultimately I pulled out the path that I believed would work best for me.

On dark fall or winter days, the sky heavy with promise and meaning, a crisp breeze stinging my cheeks, I felt alive to the core. Thoughts sprang to mind with great clarity. On such days, I could make the hard choices.

On my thinking stone, I saw the wisdom of breaking up with my high school boyfriend of three years, of going away to college when money was scarce, of pursuing my goals of teaching and writing when family members were dead set against it. I chose my life's partner on that stone. I decided when to bring my children into the world on that stone. These are a few of the more significant decisions that came to me in that special place.

Of course, people have told me that it wasn't the stone at all, that an inanimate rock couldn't possibly have anything to do with my considered conclusions, my method of selection. But I know better.

My beloved grandmother is gone now, her property sold, the stone removed—I know not where. Yet it is still with me, just as she is still with me. When I need to think something through, even now, I can close my eyes, feel the stone beneath me, and feel my grandmother's love around me. I know that I am empowered by both, know that I can still find my way. ☺

Sisyphus

A TRIBUTE TO THE ISLAND OF THASSOS

Mark G. Schroer

To these stone hills
We are but a speck
Here even the trees and grass
Serve poorly as a coat,
A torn mantel hiding no flesh.
Though we pride ourselves more
We are the scorpions
Who live in the cracks,
Piling stones for walls
Covering our heads with slate.
Still, our rafters weather and rot.
So too our life for the effort
Tumbles back low with those stones
That rise high again
For yet another.

My Mother's Path

Kim Runciman

WHEN I WAS YOUNG, I DISCOVERED THAT MY parents, to my utter bewilderment, were rock hounds—those people who stop their cars at some rocky hill or streamside pullout, take out a small pick, and chip away at things that, to my eyes, look like big heaps of nothingness. Down in our basement, my parents' sizeable collection of rocks gathered decades of dust, cobwebs, and dirt. Other than the rare need for a piece of fossil or chunk of crystal for science class, we never looked at the rocks again until long after my mother died and my father moved to a retirement center.

Fortunately, as we cleared away the detritus of our lives in the house, we found a cousin who was interested in the rock collection. The obsidian, petrified wood, agates, thunder eggs, and trilobites all found a good home. I didn't know, though, that my mother had gathered stones of a less glamorous kind for years after she'd given up the rock hounding that created the collection.

By the front walkway lay a tiny garden area filled, after years of neglect, with horsetails and desiccated bluebell stalks. It was covered in large, round, flat stones, all of which had been there forever, it seemed. I'd never thought about where they came from or who put them there.

One day I asked Dad if I could take all the garden rocks home to my own garden space. He mentioned that Mom had picked up those stones over the years on trips we'd taken, none of which I remembered.

In the back yard, in a faded, chipped, and cracked plastic pot, I found another little collection, this one of red stones and agates, milk- and moonstones, fool's gold, and other strange pebbles she'd gathered. Dad said they were just rocks she picked up and put in her pocket if she liked how they looked. That much I remembered, but I had no idea she'd kept them all those years.

I took the pot home with me that night and spread out the pebbles in a small circle on the rock pathway I was gradually creating. All the rock-hound rocks we had found in the basement were indoor rocks—the kind to look at, admire, or put on a shelf. But these little pebbles were outdoor rocks. They could withstand the rain and sun and my own feet, and they had been treasures only to my mother.

I liked them because they were all of a color scheme: pinkish and reddish, creamy, earthy whites, tan and gold. They made a lovely pocket in my long, river-like pathway filled with ordinary gray stones I'd dug up while creating planting beds.

Over the months, as I helped Dad get ready to move out, I took the larger garden stones home with me. Each one was bigger than my hand, sometimes both my hands, usually flat, and gray or white. I loved how smooth they were to the touch, how solid and heavy they felt.

In my garden, they made a small path through the flowers. I imagined that she would like this—that by keeping her stones, I was keeping part of her house and her memories, even if I didn't know where those memories came from.

Some of the stones are unusual—one is shell pink, ridged, and flecked with gold; another is deep gray with white striping that resembles letterforms. I mixed and matched them so that the path had its own visual style. Mom was more of an artist than she ever gave herself credit for being, and I think she'd like the pattern I made. There were other things of hers I took from the house—rare irises, peonies, arts and crafts—but it was the stones, surprisingly, that had the most meaning. Some of them I put next to the *Daphne odora* we'd been given as a gift at her funeral; it seemed fitting that they ringed the flowers I thought of as hers.

I had forgotten this part of her life until now. I had forgotten that occasionally Mom would take me to local neighborhood rock shows and oooh and ahh over the geodes on display. The two of us hadn't been close until I was well into adulthood, years after I'd moved out of the house, and those sorts of activities we could do only after we'd both changed. Somehow I had lost what those times meant to me. I had utterly forgotten that on my first trip to England, the things I brought back that she loved most were rocks from a shingle beach on the Dorset coast.

Her garden stones brought it all back: the insignificant that suddenly becomes important in the face of loss.

Sometimes I stand on the stones now, or look at the pebbles that don't quite blend with the rest of the path, and I remember her—usually on a beach somewhere, cold winds blowing off a northwest coast, explaining how to find agates. She roamed, head down, and I followed, holding up stone after stone, never quite getting it right. I remember mostly that I was cold and bored, and therefore cranky and less than enthused about this passion for stupid little rocks.

On occasion, I've had the chance to trot out my knowledge of rocks; people often seem surprised or impressed by what I know. In truth I know next to nothing—it's all information haphazardly recalled from random conversations, time spent barely listening when I didn't appreciate what she was passing on to me.

That's the thing that connects me to the stones I took from the house, more than their tactile quality, more than their color or shape. They are timeless. They have passed on to me a part of Mom that I didn't understand then; they are history and connection to something I've lost. They will still be somewhere in the world long after I've gone. When I touch them, I'm touching her life, and my life with her. ℮

Mother Stone

J. P. Dancing Bear

I have a piece of the Earth
Mother's heart in my pocket—
smooth, polished and warm.
A guardian bear painted
on its surface. It is a comfort
to my fingers—keeps me connected—
close to the earth. I who was born
of her mud and tears, a servant
of the earth, a caretaker
to the mother of origins,
beneficiary of her fruit,
child of her labors.
I am everything for her.
My ego disappears
with consideration of her.

I have a stone of mother heart
and when my work is done,
it will lead my ashes
back to her.

Only Stones for Throwing

Jeanie Wilson

COLD IS THE SHADED AREA BY THE REMAINS OF my great-great-grandmother's sod dugout home, and cold are the five stones I roll and massage in the palm of my right hand. In my mind's eye, the stones, smooth and worn, carry me back to a time and place, familiar yet foreign—a time and place born out of my father's childhood memory.

It was during the time of the Great Depression in a small Norwegian community called Lapland in the Flint Hills of Kansas. Food and money were scarce. After school each day, my father's Grandma Olson would dole out one bullet to my father and his brother. My father, the older of the two brothers, carried the twenty-two rifle loaded with the single bullet.

Each day those boys shot and bagged one rabbit, supper for eight: Grandma and Grandpa Gilbert Olson; Grandpa's son, Elmer Lee, and wife, Denzel; and their four children, Elmer Ray, Lee Austin, Frances June, and Mary Ann—three generations in one household.

Let out from school, the two boys picked up their bullet and rifle and headed for the woods. They knew the family's land like the backs of their hands: worn trails through the forests, low areas in the rivers and creeks for crossing, paths their grandmothers had hacked with scythes from one home to another, and hilltops with a view for miles. Seasons colored the land.

Only Stones for Throwing

My dad tells a story about a winter day. Finding a rabbit was not always easy, but for Elmer and Lee it was a time to roam the land and explore. This particular afternoon was brutally cold. The boys' winter coats were thin, so they moved quickly to keep warm. Wind had drifted the snow. Sun shafted through the trees and caused the snowdrifts to glisten and blind their eyes.

The trick to rabbit hunting was to know the rabbit and where it hid. The boys explored tree trunks with knotholes and any visible burrows. They also devised a way to slide down snowy embankments using their feet as rudders. Jackrabbits often burrowed into the snow and ground with only the tips of their ears showing.

On this day Elmer and Lee carried rounded stones in their coat pockets. The boys rushed down a snow bank, flushing out a rabbit from its frozen burrow. With the rabbit on the run, both boys hurled stones at their prey and soon discovered that a hard stone would just as easily stun or kill a rabbit with a solid hit on the head as a bullet. That day's bullet they put back for the weekend. This arrangement not only put meat on the table but also gave the boys leftover bullets they could use for a little fun, hunting possum and turkey buzzards on Saturdays.

The boys skinned the rabbits, but Grandma Olson butchered and cooked them. My father said things went along pretty smoothly until one day Grandma Olson said, "By the way, Elmer and Lee, where you been shooting those rabbits?"

Both boys stopped cold in their tracks and thought long and hard. They looked at each other and Elmer said, "In the eye. Yes, ma'am. In the eye." After all, he thought, a bullet could go clean through a rabbit's eye. That explanation seemed to settle the issue.

The next day after school, the boys came to Grandma Olson for their daily bullet for rabbit hunting. She rocked steadily on the porch for a quiet moment. From behind her back she pulled out a burlap sack containing a few stones and handed the sack to the boys without a word.

Elmer and Lee took the sack of stones, asking no questions about how Grandma Olson caught on to their scheme. That afternoon they walked miles through the snow, crisscrossing the farm several times. What was easy most days was more difficult on this afternoon. The boys began to wonder if their Grandma had told their secret to the rabbits.

Only after stalking countless rabbits did the boys kill one to bring home for supper after dark. They had used up almost all of the stones. Eventually, the boys' grandmother reverted to providing one bullet a day for hunting.

My father kept that sack with five stones in it. In my childhood, sometimes in the winter, he would bring out the sack of stones for my sister, brother, and me and tell us the story about bagging a rabbit with stones. After we held the stones, he took them back for safekeeping. Late in the afternoon, I would see him rolling and massaging the stones in his hands before placing them back in the worn burlap sack. ⌒

Stone Fruit

Philip Miller

You said you picked them
Out of a river down in the Ozarks,
Bringing them home
In a bucket like a bunch
Of potatoes and onions.
I set them in the garden
Watering them often
So they would glisten
Their earthy stains
The way they must have looked
Under the water
Where you waded in
To harvest them,
These pieces of mountain,
Refined by sand and water
To round little treasures
To blink and gleam
Beside the marigolds
And zinnias
In the garden.
Just what it needed, I said,
Holding a smooth stone
Up to my cheek,
One the size of an apple,
Cool and round and ancient.

A Stone from Ground Zero

Rev. Robert Pagliari, C.Ss.R., Ph.D.

WHEN YOU WORK FOR AN AGENCY THAT PROVIDES counseling, housing assistance, job training, and a host of other social services, you can bet there will be people lined up around the corner when disaster strikes. After the attacks of September 11, 2001, there was one heck of a line outside our building here in Manhattan. We weren't prepared for it. Who could have known?

Three months after the Twin Towers fell, a friend who had an inside connection with the NYPD asked me if I wanted to visit Ground Zero. Honestly, I didn't. The West Side Highway was still impassable. The fires were still burning out of control. The search for bodies was still a twenty-four-hour ordeal. No one without special clearance was allowed anywhere near the area. Given the explicit details I had heard in the media, I wondered why people would *want* to go there unless they absolutely had to.

My friend said, "We *have* to go. You owe it to the people who are coming to you for help. You should have firsthand experience of the hell they've suffered. That way, if they ask, you can say 'Yes, I've been down there. I've seen the devastation. And I'm sorry for what you've been through.'"

So, for the sake of the folks standing in line, we went to the center of the heartache. We took a taxi. Eight blocks away, we had to get out of the cab and walk the rest of the way. From there, the streets were reserved for emergency vehicles only.

At five blocks out there were no more discernable sidewalks—just caked mud, ash heaps, and deep tire tracks left by the continuous stream of dump trucks hauling away debris.

The distinct odor began to be perceptible when we were three blocks away. I can't describe it. But it was so thick and unusual I couldn't help mentioning it to my guide. "They call that the *World Trade Center smell*," he said softly.

We kept silent after that. We were walking on hallowed ground now: an inner-city graveyard without headstones or tombs; a cratered cemetery filled with activity, but nevertheless a most sacred place; sixteen acres of earth that had been consecrated by blood and tears.

Where once stood two pillars of strength, there was only a crippled cavern of twisted metal. Steam shovels surrounded the hole, clawing ever so gently into its basin. Specially trained dogs kept vigil alongside each crane. They sniffed every bucket that came to the surface to ensure that no piece of human remains would be missed and accidentally carried off as garbage.

We entered a dark office on the south edge of the pit. Covering one whole wall was a blueprint-type map of the property outside. Red stick-pins marked spots where identifiable bodies had been found. Tiny white flags bearing the names of the still-missing rescue workers were pressed into their "last known location."

My friend introduced me. The captain looked exhausted.

"You want to see the sky view?" he asked.

My friend nodded, "If you have time, Chief."

"Yeah, I could use a break," he muttered. "Beep me if you need me, Wilson," he spoke over his shoulder to his second-in-command as we exited the makeshift headquarters.

We walked half a block to a building on the circumference of the site and entered via a secluded loading dock. A maintenance man opened the door to a small service elevator, waited for us to press in, drew the bent safety gate down, and pushed a number.

"It can't reach the tenth floor anymore," he said out of the corner of his mouth as the elevator screeched upward. "But I can get you to nine. From there you'll have to walk up one flight and then you can step out onto the overlook. Watch your footing. There's a lot of loose stuff hanging down and piles you'll have to climb over to get outside."

I thought the elevator ride was scary until the door opened. Broken ceiling tiles, bare wires, cracked walls, and some charred metal cabinets covered with plastic were all that remained in this dank corridor. We followed the chief's flashlight, stepping over shards and squeezing around cluttered corners till we came to a staircase. We made our way slowly up one flight and then out onto a balcony, or what used to be a balcony. Here, the floor was a temporary plank of plywood that creaked as we leaned against the railing. We were ten stories high, peering directly into the jaws of an open wound.

Except for the twisted steel, the northeast corner of Ground Zero resembled a cutaway cross section of an archeological dig. We could see below street level into layers of floors that had once been shops and subway landings and parking garages below ground.

"See this hotel next to us?" The chief pointed to our left. "When the towers came down, they piled up against it, forty feet high. Until last week we couldn't even walk around the perimeter. We had to smash the windows on this side of their building, walk through their lobby, and then step through the windows on the other side."

Then he motioned to the taller structure on our right. "We found remains of bodies on the roof of that building. Probably some of the passengers in the plane that hit the south tower." His face fell into a gray expression of helplessness.

"We found Martinez over there and Jacobson there. But I think if we start digging around that area we should find three more . . ."

His voice trickled to a whisper, and the weary gloom washed over his face once again. "They must have been over there," he muttered, shaking his head with the concern of a parent whose teenagers have stayed out too late. I began to realize that this "break" from his office down below wasn't really a break for the captain after all.

"I need to be getting back," he sighed. We said a short prayer, and the three of us retraced our steps, single file, to the rickety elevator and descended to the street. It occurred to me that I would never pass along the rim of Ground "Hero" again; never in this state of destruction.

At that moment I glanced down and spied a tiny stone in our path. As I bent forward to rescue the small memorial from the mud, I asked, "May I keep this, sir?" I wasn't expecting a refusal. But in my heart I felt I needed permission to take anything away from this sacred place, even this small pebble.

The captain nodded and said, "We've never found a chunk of concrete bigger than a basketball. Can you believe that?" Then, in more somber tones he added, "And there was never a speck of wood. Never. All those office buildings, 220 floors altogether, filled with desks, tables, and bookcases galore, but not a splinter of wood survived. Just twisted steel and bits and pieces of rock, that's all."

Today the little WTC stone sits on my desk. It is a source of healing, strength, and comfort. Not only is it a remembrance of all the innocent lives that were lost on September 11, 2001, and the heroes who died trying to save them, but also an inspiration for poetry, music, prayers, and more.

For example, I never would have guessed that a little granite rock could serve as a daily reminder to be gentle with everyone I meet. It reminds me how quickly and capriciously people can be taken away. I look at it whenever work and worries seem overwhelming, and I become patient and calm. Duties and deadlines that once loomed as mountainous as skyscrapers quickly get reduced to molehills.

And when love and support appear distant, I recall how cherished I truly am when I hold it in the palm of my hand. Growing up, I was told "life is short, so whatever good you can do . . . do it." I *do good* now, as much as I can, every day. The lines around our building have dissolved from being a *task* to presenting an *opportunity* for loving my neighbor as myself. All from a sacred stone I wish I had never met, but am grateful to cherish. ℂ

Limestone Legacy

Carolyn A. Hall

When we build, let us think that we build forever. Let it not be for present delight nor for present use alone. Let it be such work as our descendants will thank us for; and let us think, as we lay stone on stone, that a time is to come when those stones will be held sacred because our hands have touched them, and that men will say, as they look upon the labor and wrought substance to them, "See! This our father did for us."

—John Ruskin,
Audels Carpenters and Builders Guide #1

IF YOU'VE EVER TRAVELED THROUGH CENTRAL Kansas, you've noticed the distinct lack of trees. My grandfather, a talented carpenter by trade and a stonemason by necessity, built the home I grew up in out of limestone rock he hand-quarried from our pasture. I saw it as a castle on the plains, a fortress against the elements. Grandpa's stones have been a calming influence for as long as I can remember. Even though we lived in Tornado Alley, an apt nickname for our part of the Midwest, I never feared windstorms.

"Your grandpa built this house to last," Mom said. "The tornadoes may take the roof, but we're safe inside these limestone walls. Grandpa built these walls three feet thick to protect us."

Over the years I watched a windmill topple, heard the wood-framed barn collapse, and helped clean up debris from a wheat granary, but the house withstood it all. That legacy made it much harder to accept the nightmare we faced when my husband and I built our first house; "survived the tempest" would better describe the ordeal.

We had to hire a company that restores houses ravaged by fire to repair the problems and damage that our builder left for us to fix. Missing walls, large drafty gaps, and dangerous stairs were just a few of the problems. One final project, the patio outside the walkout basement door, waited years for completion.

Our house sat too low in the ground, which created a water drainage problem that had to be addressed before we could proceed. It needed a fieldstone patio with drain tiles buried underneath to carry away the water. This made the project cost prohibitive. It ended up on our to-do list, but I couldn't find the motivation to begin the overwhelming chore.

Browsing at a local bookstore, I found a book on stonescaping that emphasized the use of rocks in landscaping as a means of reconnecting with nature. I smiled as I recalled my grandfather's stonework. I remembered the towering red barn we'd lost to a tornado. It had a three-tier limestone foundation my grandfather had quarried and stacked. As a young girl, my eyes had followed the level rows of fossil-filled rocks as he laid stone upon stone. I knew that's what needed to be done now to overcome the monumental task of my patio: build it one stone at a time.

I called my sister, Rose, who now owns the farm, and asked if we could have some of the stone from the old barn foundation.

"If you can find them, you can have them. Remember, they're covered with forty years of dirt and debris," she said.

My husband and I made the five-hour trek to retrieve the 100- to 200-pound rectangular rocks. Luckily, the loamy soil was easily swept away to reveal the once-sun-bleached stones. With large iron pry bars, we loosened the rocks and leveraged them onto a two-wheeled dolly. Together, we pulled them up the ramp and onto the trailer.

As we took each rock from its resting place, I felt the presence of my grandfather. The gusty Kansas wind curled the dirt around us, parched our lips, and stung our eyes, and I imagined the same dust clouds must have swirled around Grandpa the day he placed these stones. I savored the thought that we both had toiled in this same section of earth and our hands had touched the same rough-hewn rocks. His craftsmanship, still evident after decades of neglect and shifting soil, filled me with pride.

Each corner of the old foundation still held its mitered angle. The courses of stone were level, with their shim rocks in place, evening out the imperfections in the stones. I sensed the care in my grandfather's handiwork as I traced the rock surface and imagined him measuring and positioning each slab to build a solid foundation. This was his family's homestead, meant to be passed down through generations, as was his craftsmanship. I recalled the lines of John Ruskin, from *Audels Carpenters and Builders Guide #1*, the book my grandfather had studied and left to my mother who in turn gave it to me. "And let us think as we lay stone on stone, that a time is to come when those stones will be held sacred because our hands have touched them." Yes, these were truly sacred stones, gifts from my grandfather left to me as tools to rebuild my trust, and heal my home.

These stones would bring healing and protection for his descendants from the storm of poor workmanship that had shattered our lives—as devastating as any summer tornado.

I felt his guidance as I placed the stones in their new domain. The rocks told me where they belonged. They each seemed to have a predestined location, much like the pieces of a jigsaw puzzle. Learning from his example, I carefully positioned and leveled each one.

Today, a sense of well-being permeates our house. The dwelling has finally become our home. As I sit on my patio and the earthen smell of limestone hovers in the cool evening air, I hear my grandfather's voice whisper, "See! This I did for you." ◠

Barefoot

Timothy Pettet

No thoughts, only rocks

in my hands. In my shoulders, sun,

up the back of my neck, off

the rims of my ears.

       No thoughts,

in my eyes tall wild flowers

the color of pink clover,

three kinds of butterflies, blue sheen

of black wasp. Grasshoppers

surround my toes.

       No thoughts,

only the memory of limestone in the ditch

beside the road that rings the lake,

host to a stretch of setting sun,

highway of light.

Stones for the Journey

Nancy Vorkink

I REMEMBER WALKING ON AN ISLAND BEACH AMONG unpolished gray stones. Smooth, round, variable in shape and tint.

Growing up, I often visited these stone beaches in Maine. I went to college, lived overseas, married, and divorced. As time passed with its journeys and trials, and my hair turned silver, similar to the streaks in some of the older stones, I visited the island less frequently. Yet I always carried a gray stone with me, in my purse, when I went to other lands. The unpolished stone represented a place in nature and in myself where I felt comfort and tranquility.

In my daydreams, I thought more of my growing-up years on these grassy and stony island beaches. The evergreen forests were still emerald and thick in my mind. I began to miss the beaches, the Atlantic, and the climb over all these hard stones to catch a wave rolling in.

On the east side of the island, my family and I took picnics and hiked down to the secluded stone beach. We sat on the hard stones beside a huge granite boulder that tucked in a tidal pool. Tidal-pool gazing was popular after we ate our crabmeat sandwiches and chips. I saw myself as a younger woman climbing gracefully over the stones and hugging the stone boulder.

The heavy ocean mist saturated my hair, and I skipped pebbles into the incoming waves. I felt so free. I saw lobster boats dance in the distance. I felt so much peace there; I felt so connected to natural things. I rejoiced at the beauty of the world.

Rejuvenated, with all my senses alive from touching, walking, experiencing the magical stones on the beach, I marveled how the stones, the ocean, the evergreens fit together in a sacred circle. I could face city life again after my visits to the island.

In my Denver apartment, I have a bunch of beach heather, plus bleached sand dollars, blueberry jam, a toy lobster, and books on Maine. A few stones remain that were painted many years ago by my nephews: painted rocks of lighthouses, lobsters, and sailboats.

But the unpolished gray stones are my favorites. They give me the most meaning, the most comfort. Most of them lie together in a Turkish copper bowl and seem to like the light of the Colorado sky. I cherish these stones in memory of the happy times. ◯

Stones of Remembrance

Kathaleen McKay

At the going down of the sun and in the morning
We will remember them.
—Laurence Binyon, "For the Fallen"

I STARE AT AN OLD PHOTOGRAPH OF A YOUNG MAN dressed in military uniform, kneeling beside his eldest brother's headstone. The two brothers are my uncles, born three years apart; both served in the Canadian Forces during World War II. Uncle Doug, a piper with the Black Watch, safely returned home, while Uncle John, a member of the Royal Canadian Air Force, rests in Germany's Reichswald Forest War Cemetery, along with thousands of others buried there. He died at the age of twenty.

To my knowledge, Uncle Doug is the only relative to have visited John's grave. There is no date written on the back of this photo, the identity of the photographer remains a mystery, and the inscription on John's stone can barely be deciphered. Yet the expression on Doug's lean face, and his caring posture as he kneels beside the stone that bears his brother's name, speak of a powerful bond of brotherly love. Sacred memories . . . sacred stones.

Throughout human history, in cultures both ancient and contemporary, we have chosen stone to honor those held precious in life and in memory. At Reichswald, as with many other Commonwealth War Grave cemeteries, a large white Stone of Remembrance and a stone Cross of Sacrifice create a lasting tribute to those buried there.

Five words of honor appear on these monuments, chosen by Rudyard Kipling: "Their Name Liveth For Evermore." Sacred words . . . sacred stones.

A couple of years ago, on Remembrance Day (the Canadian version of Memorial Day), I decided to take a message to the woods in honor of my Uncle John, whom I had never met. My mother was fourteen when the family received news of the plane crash over Duisburg, Germany, that killed him and six other members of his crew.

Although Mom rarely expressed her sorrow in words, she kept a picture of John in his air force uniform, and for years it never moved from that same wall. She also never missed the Remembrance Day ceremony on television. It was a day she held close to her heart—a sacred day.

I searched through a collection of river rocks I'd saved to find three that invited me to use them for my ritual of remembrance. I felt guided to write one word on the smooth surface of each rock. With the stones in my pocket, I hiked through the woods until I found a beautiful place near a stream. I took the stones out of my pocket and said a prayer.

As I held the weatherworn stones in my palm, I thought of their beauty and enduring quality. The quiet moments felt sacred, as I prayed for all families who experienced the loss of loved ones. My thoughts returned to Uncle John as I carefully arranged my three stones on the ground, to be cradled once more by the earth they came from. Their words echoed the thoughts of my heart: "Lest We Forget."

Birdshot

Heather Sharfeddin

I WAS ONLY EIGHT OR NINE WHEN I FOUND IT. I always followed my father, plodding barefoot behind him in the damp, black dirt he carved up with his tiller. Looking. Often I came into possession of little scraps of bone or other artifacts whose provenance my imagination alone recognized. But on this late spring day, along the eastern end of the plot where he would put up his beanpoles, I found what I'd been looking for.

It was small. An inch long, maybe. I didn't take it for a stone at first, due to its unusual color. But it *was* a stone, pink as a baby's bootie. Only the tip emerged for my eye to stumble on. I dug it out of its grave, wiped the soil away on my new yellow shorts, and gasped with delight.

"Look!" I shouted. "Look, I found an arrowhead!"

My father, who'd already turned at the end of the row and was passing me in the other direction, paused. He didn't turn the tiller off straight away, surely preparing a fatherly nod at whatever I'd plucked up with fascination. Finally the motor stopped, leaving a roar of silence in its wake. He stood close, bent low. Studied my stone. Felt the fine sharp edges, chiseled away by a precise hand.

"Huh," he said.

"It's an arrowhead," I informed him.

"A birdshot. Nez Perce."

My family made a regular hobby of hunting up evidence of ancient civilizations in our remote area of west central Idaho. We'd go on *tipi ring* excursions, searching the grassy slopes above the Salmon River for flattened-off discs arranged in circular patterns, scanning until our eyes hurt. Or we'd climb the steep canyons overlooking the Snake River to gaze on the petraglyphs, whose origin was mysterious and muddled.

I partook of these activities with wonder and enthusiasm. But I flatly did not understand my connection to those people until I stood with my bare feet planted in the very dirt they trod, holding that arrowhead. As my father was tilling the earth, preparing to sow the seeds that would feed our family, I was holding in my hand another man's tool to feed his. I got that. Right then.

I live in the suburbs now. I'm grown and have a child of my own. I didn't really choose to live in the suburbs, but didn't happen upon the luck to remain in the remote West that shaped my childhood and still captivates my imagination.

But I still have that little pink birdshot arrowhead. It is among the few treasures I would be hard-pressed to part with. And sometimes, when I watch the evening news, witness the fighting and violence—the clash of nations, clash of races—I think of that stone.

Once in a while I take it out and examine it again, remembering that we're all tethered to this planet by the same needs. I fancy that when one Nez Perce Indian chipped this rock into a tool for the good of his family, the world was a simpler place. Then I look again at my arrowhead and realize it's my idea that is simple—that a clash of cultures made it an object of my wonder to begin with. But perhaps if we listen carefully to what this little stone can teach us, the world ahead *can* be a simpler place. ☺

Petrified Forest

Tony D'Arpino

The arrowhead
Lay with the other colored stones
In the local brook

The hunter lost it
Or found the heart
Of an animal
And prayed
To pass through it
To the dry locust shells beyond

Now in the hands
Of another hunter
I add the arrowhead
To my small collection

Like the stones themselves
Collecting them
Is a slow process
A petrified forest
Traveling in a child

From the Ground Up
Deborah Shouse

WHEN I FIRST INVESTED IN A GEM AND MINERAL shop, I didn't think I'd be managing the store. I didn't know anything about rocks, except that I had enjoyed picking them up when I was a kid. I was a businesswoman ready for a different kind of business. For the past decade, I'd worked night and day in a highly demanding health-care enterprise. I dealt with staff, patients, vendors, inspectors, and issues. I loved the work, but I wanted something less fierce, less time-consuming.

A rock shop sounded charming. The doors would calmly get locked at 5:00 P.M., and I wouldn't feel like I was "between a rock and a hard place."

My manager was an accomplished collector. She stocked the shop with gorgeous and esoteric specimens from all over the world. Those specimens were museum quality—in fact, I ended up donating them to a museum when all too soon I discovered not many people wanted to buy them.

People wanted gifty gems, sparkly stones, dramatic rocks. By default I got involved in restocking and working in the shop. That's when my customers began teaching me about the power of stones.

Jay was my first teacher. When he first appeared, I was scared of his big dirty black coat and the wild look in his eye. He raced over to the amethysts and began holding them, one by one. "I work in food service," he told me. "You know what Shakespeare said about food service?"

I did not.

"'Why, then, the world's mine oyster. Which I with sword will open,'" he said, bowing from the waist with panache.

"I need an amethyst to give me energy," he continued. "Amethyst has a vibration that gives you wisdom and helps you intuit what you're supposed to do. Plus, it's a de-stressor. This is the right one for me."

He opened his hand and showed me a smooth amethyst stone.

I drew closer. This was interesting—a poet who worked in food service who needed an amethyst.

"How do you know it's the right one?" I asked.

"By the way I feel when I'm holding it," he informed me.

After Jay left, I went over to the amethysts and held one in each hand. Eenie, meenie, the old childhood rhyme marched through my head. Which one would I choose?

I didn't know. I picked another two and still couldn't tell any difference.

Mary taught me about quartz crystals. She bought lovely clusters to put around her bedroom. "I'm healing from a broken relationship," she told me.

Elinor taught me about fluorite. She used the translucent purple-and-green stone to put herself in a state of openness.

A woman bought a handful of unpolished garnets, which give safety to the traveler. Another woman bought a chunk of pink rose quartz, to bring love into her life. A man bought a tiger's eye for protection, strength, and courage.

One by one, my customers showed me what I was standing in the middle of—an earthy energetic wonderland, a place of discovery and connection, a haven of healing and beauty.

I began buying rocks for myself, giving them as gifts. I explored the feel, the color, and the energy of them.

No single rock has changed my life, not yet at least. My relationship with rocks has grown slowly, a series of discoveries and pleasures, adding a depth and intricacy to my days, connecting me deeper with people, with myself, and with the unending richness of the earth. ☍

Visiting the Stone Shop

Beverly Partridge

She is no surprise.
Others like her dwell
in little shops
elsewhere,

flashy smooth earrings,
though she is not flashy,
you could pass her
on the street.

She sits behind a counter
on a high stool,
unhurried, grading papers
or writing her memoirs.

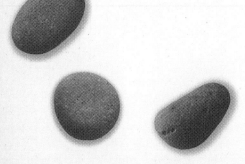

Small bowls filled
with glittering stones,
quinacridone violet
diarylide yellow,

surround her.
Translucent white
moon eggs from China,
leopardskin jasper,

garnet and bloodstone
bring their mysteries
from Asia. As I circle
my way through her treasures,

she does not look up once.
How do you sell past dreams
that fit softly in your hand?

Touchstone

Patricia Clothier

STANDING ON THE LIMESTONE STEPS LEADING FROM our cabin, I see a copse of dogwood covered with white blooms framing the rich browns of the creek bank. Lacy ferns hang between boulders. Native columbines tremble as a sudden breeze stirs the willows. Clumps of wild blue Sweet William nod beside Indian paintbrush.

Deer Creek runs by one side of our land while a rugged country road winds along the north border. Here on a wooded slope hides a rustic cabin covered with weathered siding and wearing a tin roof capped by a chimney for its old wood stove. Flat stones carried from the nearby creek make a path to the front door.

One of these flat rock steps is an Indian grinding stone, a *metate,* turned over to conceal the worn cavity. I put it here as a hiding place for an extra cabin key and to keep it from theft. When I first found the *metate* at the top of our ridge, I left it where I found it under an old oak. A few days later I went back, but it was missing. Scanning the area, I spied it some fifty yards distant. A poacher, it seems, had moved it that far, turned it over, and intended to return later to steal the artifact. This time, I carried the stone back to the cabin for safekeeping.

When I look at this oblong piece of limestone, I think of the Osage Indians who camped on this land. They came here to the Missouri Ozarks on hunting-and-gathering trips in the spring and fall. They built temporary huts smaller than their permanent longhouses.

The native women pulverized seeds and corn on this mortar to nourish the tribe. The men hunted bear and beaver in the spring and buffalo and deer in the fall. The women cured the hides, wove mats, and gathered edible plant foods. After the first frost, the squaws made and dried flat cakes from persimmon pulp. They also ground boiled corn and pounded it on the grinding stone into a fine meal for later use.

Women had an important part in Osage life. In addition to preparing food, they made most of the essential home items and even constructed the homes. They sewed clothing from animal skins and made household utensils.

In my mind, I see these natives collecting water from the spring-fed creek as it dashes over shelves of flat stones and forms shallow pools. The women wade in the creek and paint the part in the young girls' hair red to give courage for that day.

My girls, Candy and Jaime, wade here today and chase silver minnows or rust-speckled crawdads that dart back to shelter under a fallen hickory log. The morning sun halos their hair as they make lazy-floating boats of wild lupines.

Later I climb the hill behind the cabin. The rich loam feels spongy as I pass beneath twisting oak trees. Patches of warm sunlight bounce on the gray stillness of the stones. A wild rose tugs at my jeans. The sweet fragrance of its soft pink blossoms mingles with the earthy smells of lichens and mulch.

There is no stink of the factory here, no clang of the city, no sign of hurry and worry. Instead, the quiet rustle of sycamore branches brings a peaceful feeling and the hope of a waiting pot of stew.

When I return to the suburbs, I carry the grinding stone with me to place it in my garden. Here, it is safe from thieves. Here others will enjoy it, a symbol of the strong, vigorous Indians who used the rock so many generations ago. The worn-away trough in the rock will fill with rainwater and draw birds, chipmunks, and squirrels to drink, another reward of unadorned Nature. The grinding stone is my touchstone, reminding me of a simpler, more peaceful life.

Caution: Women at Work

Karla Linn Merrifield

They are yet in my fingertips, those
Archaic women of Seminole Canyon,
their earnest breath as they pounded
sotol bulbs into flour on a smooth
flat stone oiled to a patina enduring
eight thousand years seeped deeply
into pores of my hand as it caressed
the sandstone surface of what in my age
would be a Formica countertop, also
waist high. So, yes, they are still in my wrists
& forearms, my shoulders responding with
an ache from the vibrations of their exertions.

Can't you hear their mashing, smashing against
such a strong stone at cavern's edge,
the ancient brown women of short stature?
& their gossip as two of them labor over paddles
of juicy prickly pear cactus, whose husband
is the better artist of pictographs that one day
three-hundred-twenty generations later
will draw tourists from distant regions
to stare & gasp at their shamanistic figures
while I stand among those travelers but
transfixed by an afterimage of what we now
disparage as women's work, theirs & mine, ours.

Moving Along

Cherise Wyneken

"YOU'LL NEED A WHOLE VAN," THE AGENT SAID after seeing what we were taking on our long move—California to Florida.

It was hard to leave behind our lovely house built on a steep hillside, and the small creek that flowed through the backyard and fell in a ten-foot waterfall. Even harder was saying goodbye to parents, children, relatives, and friends. Three thousand miles would be too far for drop-in visits. Yet, for now, my friend Charlotte was here, offering to help any way she could.

Charlotte is a woman tuned to nature. We often took walks in our neighborhood or long hikes with our children on nearby park trails. She gifted my life with treasures that she found: colorful leaves, feathers, a rose from her garden.

One day she brought me a stone from the creek bed of her family's summer home, a large, smooth oval-shaped stone that seemed to speak to me. I placed it in the front garden near the cherry tree I'd planted. Whenever I walked past it, I thought of her.

Now all that would soon be over. The van was scheduled to come Friday after Thanksgiving, and I made arrangements to fly out that night. My husband had already gone ahead. When moving day arrived, Charlotte came to see me through the trauma. The van appeared on time—half full of someone else's goods.

"We'll have to send another truck tomorrow for the rest of it," the driver said.

"I can't wait until tomorrow," I replied frantically. "I have my airplane ticket for tonight."

"Don't worry," Charlotte intervened. "I'll come by tomorrow and take care of everything." A person not only tuned to nature but also to people's needs.

I was busy unpacking the first load when the second van pulled up at our new home. The last thing that must have gone on and the first thing to come off was my stone. Charlotte had rescued it from the yard. I placed it in the center of our rock garden where it sent warm vibes as I came and went—a symbol of our solid friendship.

After several years in that neighborhood, the people next door adopted a baby. Alex was a sweet child, but somehow he always seemed lonely and sad. As he grew, he loved to come across the lawn to play with the stones on our front patio. I would hear him out there, talking to himself contentedly. One day, after he had paid his usual visit to our yard, I found an empty space where my stone had been. The empty space moved to my heart as well—as though I'd lost a friend.

I debated about asking for it back when I felt a strong objection—as if the stone were saying, "It's time for me to move along. Alex needs a friend like Charlotte." ℰ

The White Rock Lady

Dru Clarke

WE HAD A SUMMER PLACE IN NEW JERSEY, WHERE I grew up, near the Delaware River. At the foot of the steep hill, where the lane scrawled through deciduous woodland up to the stone house, lay a gravel-and-cobble–bottomed creek. Native Americans once called it the Queequacomissicong. Others called it Milford Creek. We called it "our" creek.

Just upstream from the low-water bridge at the ford was a bend where another stream flowed into it; there, a large, flat rock jutted out over the riffle, a shallow reach where the water raced. I used to kneel on that rock and peer into the stream, pretending I was the White Rock Lady. (White Rock was a brand of beverage, and its icon was a beautiful fairy-like woman with diaphanous gown and wings.)

It didn't matter that the rock was brown: it was white to me. Usually I had nothing on but a pair of underpants, so it was easy to pretend I was dressed as the White Rock Lady. Something else also happened, beyond a child's imagination. That rock and stream bend are where I learned to love freely flowing water and everything associated with it.

Because I spent so much carefree time and felt such pleasure on the rock and by the stream, they became indistinguishable parts of me. I was "inside" this rock and stream, and they are inside me even today. Thinking of them now, I am viscerally connected to that childhood experience. I feel content and deeply satisfied, perhaps the way a kitten feels with a belly full of cream.

When I became a teacher of environmental and marine science, beach materials were one of my favorite tools for teaching the kids. Sands and gravels and cobbles hewn from the continents and gathered from the world's shores became the text for understanding origins and change. They represented the connectedness of land and sea and brought me back to my childhood rock and the stream that relentlessly worked on it. Eventually, a concrete ford changed the bottom of the stream where we crossed, but "my" rock upstream remained for my son and his two boys to enjoy as they were growing up.

Mother is buried in a Milford cemetery. Her gravesite, marked with a stone the color of my White Rock, is oriented so that when you stand next to it, you can look up the valley to the hills through which the creek flows. She'd like that.

Retired from the classroom, I now conduct volunteer stream studies with school children. I still look for rocks like the one I perched on in my childhood, for kids to kneel on today. My rock may no longer be at the bend of the creek, but it still exists in the riverbed that wends toward the sea, in the sands of its shores, and in my being. ℮

Meditation

STONE COLORS AND WHAT THEY MEAN

Below are some guidelines for interpreting the significance of stone colors. Meanings can vary depending on the background and tradition of the person interpreting the stones, the energy of individual stones, and many other factors. In addition to using these guidelines, always use meditation or other intuitive aids for guidance as to what colors you should use for your specific purpose.

A gemstone resource guide, such as *Love Is in the Earth: A Kaleidoscope of Crystals,* by A. Melody, or *The Illustrated Directory of Healing Crystals: A Comprehensive Guide to 150 Crystals and Gemstones,* by Cassandra Eason, is also helpful. Your local library and bookstores may offer other choices. Find the resource that fits you best.

Red: For grounding; also for enlivening, energizing at the physical or emotional level.

Examples: Ruby, red jasper, garnet

Orange: Helps clear issues related to sexuality or rekindle the romantic aspects of a relationship; also helps with making a fulfilling life-to-death transition.

Examples: Carnelian, orange calcite, mookaite

Gold, yellow: For prosperity; promotes harmony in the workplace; protects against negative people.

Examples: Amber, yellow jasper, topaz, yellow calcite, yellow fluorite

Peach, salmon: Promotes family harmony and communication.

Examples: Coral, chalcedony, unakite

Green: For personal healing and growth; also gradually attracts money or good fortune.

Examples: Turquoise, emerald, moldavite, jade

Blue: Helps you see beyond the immediate reality; helps connect with angels and spirit guides.

Examples: Lapis lazuli, sapphire, azurite, aquamarine

Rose, pink: Enhances feelings of love. Rose quartz is universally known as the stone of love.

Examples: Rhodachrosite, danburite, rhodonite, pink tourmaline, rose quartz

Purple: For enhancing and recharging energies, enhancing psychic abilities, an overall healing color; also lowers tension levels and promotes harmony in the home.

Examples: Amethyst, purple fluorite, sugilite, lepidolite, charoite

Brown: For personal protection, regeneration, and stability.

Examples: Leopardskin jasper, tiger's eye, mahogany obsidian

Black: Absorbs negative vibrations, hostility, and stress. Many black stones have strong grounding properties.

Examples: Black onyx, obsidian, tektite

White or clear: Amplifies healing energies, attracts positive astral energy and light; for purification.

Examples: Clear quartz, milky quartz, moonstone, diamond, white opal

Part Three

Stone Legacies:
Stories from the Great Stone Sites

SONG OF RECOGNITION
WILLIAM PITT ROOT

After the long letters
have been written, read,
abandoned, after
distances grow absolute
and speech, too,
is distance, only
listening is left.

I have heard the dark hearts
of the stones
that beat once in a lifetime.

Pilgrimage
Maril Crabtree

THE FIRST THING I NOTICE IS HOW THIS MEDIEVAL matrix of worship dominates the landscape, spreading its stone shoulders like a preening peacock. Flying buttresses, they're called, but they remind me of broad shoulders draped in the fine lace of twelfth-century stone carvings.

Chartres Cathedral has stood, proud and peerless, through centuries of wars and restless revolutions, its huge wooden doors open to everyone, its stone floors shockingly bare in contrast to the complex statuary and burst of jeweled windows lining the walls.

Tourists arrive by the busload day after day, year after year, to see this tough stone survivor. They spend a few minutes or a few hours absorbing its history, appreciating its artistry. Although Chartres gazes with benevolence on all who come, her soul belongs to those who tiptoe through the stone silence, who linger to kneel in the pews, who light candles and pray for souls long dead and souls that suffer still. To those who approach her in such reverence, she seems to whisper a special welcome.

I first saw Chartres as a college student, when I spent the summer abroad with a group of two dozen others. During the week, we stayed in Paris. We spent mornings in a Sorbonne classroom absorbing the particularities of French verb tenses. In the afternoons, we explored the grittier slang of the Boul' Mich and other Parisian streets.

On weekends, we boarded a bus and toured other areas: the castles of the Loire Valley, the coast of Normandy, the champagne vineyards, and, finally, the immense Chartres Cathedral. In those days, we girls wore skirts below the knee and high-collared blouses, and we covered our heads with scarves or handkerchiefs before entering the sanctuary—an action required by the church's Rules for Tourists.

Now, decades later, I have returned to Chartres for a reason. I've discovered the power of the labyrinth, a specific circular pattern created from stone or other material that makes a path to be slowly walked while meditating or praying. Chartres has one of the oldest labyrinths, created around A.D. 1200, carved into its stone floor. Its shape is the classic eleven-circuit design divided into four perfect quadrants with a center space. Unlike a maze, a labyrinth has one entrance and one exit. As long as you follow its path, you can't get lost or run into a dead end.

The ancient design reenacts the journey of life, at times going forward and then doubling back on itself until one loses all sense of beginning or end. But if one continues to put one foot in front of the other, faithfully following the outlined path, suddenly there is an opening to the center—to Spirit, to the heart of the journey.

Coming out of the labyrinth is not a simple retracing of one's steps. Again there is a sense of being led, of returning to the world through mysterious turnings until one finds oneself rounding the last corner into open territory. Although I have walked many labyrinths, I never fail to experience a flash of anxiety somewhere in the middle—"Am I lost? Will I really make it to the center?"—and at that moment, I feel the familiar self-doubt that accompanies me on so much of my life journey.

The Rules for Tourists have changed. Like other women, I wear slacks and a casual shirt. No head covering is required. Nevertheless, the closer I get, the more I sense an attitude of respect and awe among young and old alike.

Inside, the light is soft and dim. I am intent on finding what I came for as I step into the narrow nave flanked by rows of simple wooden chairs. Here, in the center of the stone floor, is the labyrinth. I picture the thousands upon thousands of feet that have circled its path—along with countless other penitents who made the journey on their knees.

I kneel and put my hand on the grooved stone. To touch this stone is to touch centuries of humanity: those who came to forgive and to be forgiven, to pray for world peace and to seek personal peace, to offer prayers for the sick and to be restored to health. This stone passage endowed them with a sense of hope or peace that seems to radiate from the stone itself.

As I run my hand over the stone, its warmth surprises me. How can solid stone encased in stone walls—a perfect example of the expression "stone cold"—be this warm—almost alive? I look around for someone to confirm my impression. I see an older man making his way up the aisle, leaning on a cane.

"Do you know anything about the history of the labyrinth?" I ask.

We talk about the power of this special form of contemplative movement, the circular back-and-forth pattern of walking that creates a sense of being on the path of life itself—with God, or some eternal presence, at its center.

Finally, I tell him how I found the stone floor warm to my touch.

He smiles. "It does not surprise me," he says. "I come here often to walk this path. Each experience is different. The labyrinth can be warm one time and cool the next. It can be a moving ocean, rocking me with memories, or a distant mountain that beckons me to climb."

His eyes are clear and serene, the eyes of someone who knows the mystery of life, death, and many events in between. This stranger has given me a valuable nugget of spiritual wisdom. In his words I hear an acceptance of change, of equanimity with the curves and turnings of life that embody the essence of the labyrinth walk. The labyrinth invites me to embrace my self-doubt, to keep going despite its presence until I arrive, once again, at the center.

Like stone, ever-changing yet the same through eons, I can explore my inner landscape of anxiety, fear, and doubt, and I can trust that I'm on the path leading to the center of my spiritual truth. Returning to Chartres Cathedral has given me the opportunity to return to myself. ◯

Nocturne in Blue

Barbara Crooker

She asked me to bring her back a stone
from Paris, where even the dirt is historic,
but I wanted, instead, to find her the color
of l'heure bleu, the shimmer of twilight

with the street lamps coming on, the way they keep
the dark back for just a little while, the reflections
of headlamps and taillights, red and gold, on the Champs
d'Élysees wet with rain and a fog rising.

And there's the way the past becomes a stone,
how you carry it with you, lodged in your pocket.
The blue light deepens, evening's melancholy shawl,
the wide boulevard of the Seine, the way the stones

of the monuments become watery, ripple in the currents
and the wind. Everything seems eternal here,
to us from the West, who have no memory of dates
like 52 B.C., 1066, the fin de siècle

as we barge on past the millennium,
history's crazy swirl, oil on pavement,
a promenade down les Grands Boulevards.
This is what I'd bring back: shadows of stones,

(continued on next page)

twilight longings, a handful of crushed lilacs
from the bar at the Closerie, some lavender de Provence,
Odilon Redon's chalky mauves, a jazz piano playing
  the blues,
Mood Indigo; just a condensation of blue,

distilled in a small glass bottle with a stopper,
as if it came from an expensive parfumerie,
musk of the centuries, the gathering dusk,
a hedge against night, the world that will end.

Searching for the Navel Stone

Judith Diana Winston

I DECIDED TO SPEND MY LAST DAY TOURING EASTER Island on horseback. In the morning I planned to go to Anakena Beach to photograph, in perfect light, the line of seven Moai (the famed giant stone statues scattered across the island) that I had only captured late in the day. Then I would go to Rano Raraku, the extinct volcano from which they were carved, and top it all off with a swim in the crater lake created by the volcano—a kind of mystical baptism. No one had yet charted its depth, and I secretly felt that it must have some healing properties.

Finally, I wanted to try to find an unusual round stone I had heard about. Nobody could tell me much about this stone or precisely where it was, but intuitively I sensed that it was important to see it. Aside from my intuition, the fact that it appeared to be unknown to many of the small island's inhabitants seemed reason enough to find it.

The family I was staying with warned me that I had planned too much to accomplish in one day, and that if I did want to do it all I should rent a jeep. Old habits die hard, however, and I had a romantic vision of myself riding horseback around the magical little island, the wind in my hair, experiencing my kinship with the nature spirits. Peu, a young family nephew, volunteered to accompany me as my guide.

Within an hour of "communing with nature" on horseback, my upper back muscles went into spasm. I had not ridden a horse in almost ten years, the gait was awkward, and Peu had been moving us on at a rapid clip, for fear that I would never cover my proposed itinerary before dark.

We reached our first destination, Anakena Beach, at high noon, with the sun boring down on our heads and backs. I lay down on top of a wooden picnic table in an attempt to release my back. Peu unpacked our sandwiches and drinks. The light was piercingly bright and directly overhead: so much for my perfect morning shots of the seven Moai! I felt awful. Clearly I was not going to make it to Rano Raraku, either. I couldn't hide my disappointment.

While eating our cheese sandwiches and lemonade, Peu and I discussed what to do.

"Have you ever seen the round stone your uncle told me about?" I asked. We had been given some vague directions to it.

"No, I've never been to it," said Peu. "But I think I know where to find it, and I don't think it's very far from where we are right now. Do you think you can still ride?"

I didn't know, but one way or another I understood that I was going to have to get back on that horse. This was not "civilization," where one could just go to a phone booth and call a cab. I doubt that any phones existed on this part of the island. All of the people lived in Hanga Roa, the little town on the far end, where there were phone lines and electricity. The rest of the island was considered one large open-air museum. Even agricultural pursuits were not allowed.

I settled myself back on my horse. "Let's try to find it," I said, mentally groaning and gritting my teeth.

Slowly we began to head in the direction that Peu's uncle had described. We spent hours combing back and forth over the rocky terrain, one small section at a time. To be honest, I was ready to call it all off, but Peu insisted.

"It's your last day," he said in impassioned Spanish. "If you don't see it today you will never have another chance."

I have learned that Spirit chooses strange packaging in which to clothe our teachers and guides at any given moment, so I continued the search.

By the time we actually stumbled upon the stone, I was exhausted and really in pain. I could have sworn that we had ridden over that same spot many times before, but suddenly, there it was: a perfectly round stone about sixteen inches in diameter. It lay near the broken remains of the largest of the Moai ever moved from the crater.

The place was peaceful and abnormally quiet. As I rested my fevered forehead on the cool stone, a rich, velvet blackness suddenly enveloped me and began to swirl with color. A long tunnel appeared and above its opening I saw the very stone on which I now rested my head. It looked about five times its actual size.

Surrounding the great stone were twelve Beings possessing an uncanny similarity to the Moai scattered about the island. These Beings sat in a circle and focused their great eyes on the now glowing stone. All at once they made a humming sound like a swarm of angry bees. The surrounding space was filled with shimmering geometric forms.

At the other end of the tunnel, the huge Moai, freshly carved from the crater at Rano Raraku, began to glide in solemn procession to various locations around the tiny island. Having reached their preordained spots, they positioned themselves atop the *ahi* (the stone platforms prepared for them) and became inanimate stone once again. The Moai I saw all had large eyes made of white shell and obsidian. Once in place, in all but one location, they faced not out to sea to watch for incoming vessels, but inland as if forming a ring of protection around the tiny island. Here they remained like silent sentinels, great guardians of this sacred place until they were toppled generations later by an angry people who lost their ability to access their ancient magic.

With a certain abruptness, whatever I had attuned myself to came to an end, and I returned to myself. I was shocked to find that only a few moments of clock time had passed.

Peu looked at me rather oddly. He knew that something had taken place, but he could not figure out just what it might be.

"Do you wish you could build a house here so you could wake up every day close to your stone?" he asked.

I smiled. Although Peu had lived on the island all of his twenty-six years, he had not even known the stone existed before his uncle told us about it, and had no idea how his ancestors might have used it. The oral tradition relating to the site had long since vanished.

I packed up my camera gear, and we slowly began the long trek back to the other end of the island. I was too exhausted even to think about how I was going to make it. We had ridden for about an hour into the coolness of the oncoming night when I finally felt that I could go no further.

With Peu's help, I hitched a ride with one of the few vehicles that appeared on the isolated dirt road. A local family picked me up in an old four-wheel drive truck with a covered cab. I gratefully accepted the ride, left Peu with the horses, and climbed into the back of the already crowded truck, my cameras in tow.

A blond, bearded man in his late forties or early fifties sat across from me. We smiled pleasantly at each another as we bumped along in the darkness. Suddenly I felt the bearded man's eyes lock onto my backpack camera case.

"It's a camera," I said in Spanish. He nodded silently. "I was shooting pictures at a very special place," I continued.

My Spanish is limited and I get a little nervous when I reach the outer edges of my vocabulary, which is almost always, so I generally smile and use my hands a lot when I talk. In spite of my back pain, I was smiling like crazy.

He said nothing, just kept on staring, so I felt obliged to continue talking.

"We had a hard time finding the place I was looking for and I stayed on the horse much too long," I babbled on. His stare was making me uncomfortable.

There was complete silence, except for the bumping and squeaking of the ancient vehicle as it bounced on through the night. Suddenly he whispered harshly and abruptly into the blackness, "Te Pito Kura."

"What?" I said, startled.

"Te Pito Kura!" He paused and then continued slowly, still in Spanish, "You were at Te Pito Kura."

"I was at a round stone," I said in my best accented Spanish.

"Yes," he said. "It is called Te Pito Kura, the Navel Stone. The ancient name for Rapa Nui, which you call Easter Island, is Te Pito O Te Henua, 'The Navel of The World.'"

"Oh," I said.

He paused again before continuing, this time speaking very slowly, punching up each word and enunciating it with great care to make certain that I understood.

"The ancient legends say that there is a line of energy that runs directly from Te Pito Kura to Rano Raraku, the volcano where the Moai were carved. That is how the statues were moved, you know, through the power of mind focused on Te Pito Kura. They were moved by mind and by sound." Looking directly into my eyes, he continued.

"The Moai were made to walk to their places on the *ahi.*"

He let that sink in for a moment before mumbling what sounded like, "You know that." It was definitely a statement and not a question.

Then he relaxed his posture and continued in a more conversational tone.

"I came here from Chile when I was still a boy. I wanted to uncover the mysteries of the island. I have never left."

The truck suddenly lurched to a stop. It was time to get out. With many smiles all around and the driver's refusal to take any money from me, I got out of the dilapidated little truck and off they went jogging along into the night.

The next day, on my plane ride back to Papeete, I had ample time to contemplate the Chilean's words. The concept that ancient stone sites all over the world had been created with the assistance of focused thought to alter the laws of gravity was part of some teachings I had read about. I had also run across this idea in some of the myths and legends surrounding many of the different sites.

The Chilean seemed to have appeared for the sole purpose of verifying what I had "seen" and felt, to make certain that this time I did not write it off as "just my imagination." These ancient stone figures came to stand in their places through mind-spirit technologies we no longer understand—but may someday re-create.

Note: This story is an excerpt from the author's forth-coming book, *The Keeper of the Diary,* based on more than eight years of travels photographing and experiencing many of the planet's most ancient and mysterious megalithic (great stone) sacred sites. ℮

Callanish Stone Circle

Alison Leonard

To come here asks nothing
but the shedding of protective turf
and the knowing that for stones to stand
there's one necessity: as much beneath
as is above. And no shoes.

You can greet them,
and in return they will greet you.
Think sinew, breath, retina, bone.
Bring yours, and they will speak with theirs.

Now here's the hardest shedding:
the word "only." "Only" stones.
Naked, without the "only" judgment,
you can lock eyes with each of them,
and each moment will be a millennium,
and the marrow of your bones will shimmer
as if an orchestra on the most distant star
were playing an ancestral symphony
right by your ear.

For this is where your mother
built her altar, and fashioned it
in awe to face the wind and sun and sea,
not to bow down, but to stand,
shoeless, with her own song,
at the intersection
of the above with the beneath.
She asks of you nothing
but to stand, and let
the bones of your ears pick up the song.

Journey to Stonehenge

Jennifer Goodenberger

FOR MY FORTIETH BIRTHDAY, I GAVE MYSELF THE gift of a trip to England, a lifelong dream. I had a great desire to see the standing stones and make a pilgrimage to sacred sites. People who had visited when ugly barriers surrounded the stones at Stonehenge told me to avoid it. I wanted to see it anyway.

I was totally unprepared for my reaction when I saw Stonehenge for the first time.

Driving along the gently rolling hills of the Salisbury Plain, I knew I was within sighting distance of the ancient stones, but I couldn't see them yet. I came up over a rise in the hills and thought I caught a glimpse of them, but then went back down into a valley. When the highway rose again, there the site stood before me.

I burst into tears, couldn't speak, almost couldn't breathe. I was overwhelmed by the stones, the setting, the sacredness, the very presence of something so deeply spiritual, so deeply unexplainable. Never have I had the kind of response I had in that moment.

As I stood in front of these stones, I changed. Perhaps it was to be expected that I would feel different after being deepened by exposure to the sacred. But I could never have imagined Stonehenge would change me professionally.

When I returned from England, I did a series of paintings of Stonehenge, Avebury, and other sacred stone sites in England. In the paintings I illuminated the stones with vibrant colors. Painting was a new outlet I had discovered only a month before my trip. The work that flowed through me now felt channeled. I had no technique or experience to account for the quality of the paintings. The remarkable outcome was a new career as a visual artist, something I have pursued with great success ever since.

Until then, I had been a concert pianist and composer. My piano playing changed remarkably after Stonehenge. I had left for England a classical pianist, true to the exact notes composers had written. Even my own compositions were written out note for note. But after standing within the energy of the stones, I found it hard to play other composers' music, even more difficult to play written notes. My ability to play classical music plummeted. I was almost ready to give up playing piano professionally and devote myself to the visual arts.

But my love of music and my instrument continued to speak to me. Over the next year, I performed less for the public and more for myself. My style changed to become freer and more improvisational. My fingers found new ways to caress the keys and create new sounds and harmonies.

Not only was this new style more enjoyable, but also it was easier on my body and hands. I now play with a sense of ease and joy. Compositions in this style also flowed out of me, and I released two CDs of my original quiet, sensual, meditative piano solos.

Much of my work involves compositions about the spiritual world and exploring the unconscious. I composed a piece about Stonehenge and in concert showed the paintings as I played. This eventually led to a full-length concert performance, entitled "Stones I Have

Known," which chronicled my travels to Stonehenge and other sacred stone sites in the world through original solo piano music, slides of my paintings, and poetry/prose to guide the listener through the performance.

My pilgrimage to Stonehenge brought more gifts than I ever could have imagined or dreamed. It stands as the most pivotal moment of my life. It brought an unending fascination with ancient mysteries and continues to fuel my artistic visions, creations, thoughts, research, and travels. Those few moments changed my life in a magnificent way. I am forever grateful. ☺

Khamseem and Stone

Margo Fallis

HAVE YOU EVER BEEN SO THIRSTY THAT YOU STARTED hallucinating, visualizing yourself crawling around on your hands and knees through the middle of a hot, arid desert, with sand blowing all around you? I've seen this happen in the movies, but never in my life did I think it would become a reality for me.

My mother and I went on a trip to the Holy Land with a group of fifty other people. We spent the first week touring the northern, more agricultural parts of the country and then drove south, to the desert.

Our guide, Aliyah, mentioned the next stop was Masada. Having neglected to study the geography of the Holy Land, the name meant little to me. She gave a brief account of the area's history as the bus chugged along. The road looked like a black snake meandering through a vast sea of brown sand. In this area, called the Judean Desert, the temperature outside was nearing 110 degrees Fahrenheit. It was barren and desolate. I couldn't see any plants, trees, shrubs, or flowers. I saw one animal, a surefooted goat, bleating as it clambered among the rocks.

When a massive stone tower came into view, I pushed my face against the bus window and stared. "Is that Masada?" I asked. The isolated, flat-topped rock reminded me of the mesas back home in the American Southwest. It jutted straight up from the desert floor to a height of 1,300 feet above the Dead Sea.

Aliyah continued her lecture. In Hebrew, she said, the word *masada* means "fortress" or "stronghold." I heard words like "King Herod," "fortified," "Romans," "ramp," and "suicide." I was too enthralled by what I was seeing to listen closely.

The bus stopped at a small group of buildings. The visitor's center stood among palm trees, offering shade and air conditioning. Green grass and pools of water looked out of place among the desert sands. A guide met our group and huddled us together in a room to watch a short presentation. He explained that those of us who wanted to go to the top had two choices. We could either walk up the Snake Path, an ancient and very steep serpentine trail that made its way up the side, or we could take the modern tram. I opted for the tram, as did most of the others in our group. Some, like my mother, chose to stay at the visitor's center and wait for the rest of us.

I've never enjoyed cable cars. Once I saw the height of Masada close up, I hesitated, but I knew this was probably the only chance I'd ever have. I found a place in the corner where I felt safe, and when the doors shut and the cable car began to move, I knew it was too late to change my mind.

I looked up at the cable. One large pole dangled from the steel ropes, noisily inching its way to the top. After being encouraged by the others to "enjoy the moment," I looked down on the Dead Sea. It sparkled like a blue sapphire, glistening in the sunlight, the only thing of beauty in the midst of arid desert.

When the cable car stopped, I whispered a silent prayer of thanks for making it to the top without plunging to our deaths. We poured out of the cramped car, and when I noticed we still had eighty steps to climb to reach the top, I let out a loud sigh. Most of the people in my group were elderly, and climbing was difficult for them, but stoically they went up, one step at a time.

I listened to Aliyah as we strolled from one ancient ruin to another, stopping to view the crumbling walls, towers, and gates. We entered rooms to find the floors and walls decorated with mosaics still as beautiful and colorful as the day they were laid. Ceilings painted with frescoes and fluted columns urged me to use my imagination, envisioning the people who thousands of years ago had lived high on top of this rock. Storerooms, swimming pools, bathtubs, and saunas brought this place of ruin to life for me.

This stone mountain became part of me, part of my soul.

When we moved to the ramp on the other side, Aliyah told us the story of the Romans and how they forced Jewish slaves to build it, dumping buckets and barrels of dirt in a mound, until the ramp reached the summit. I saw the battering ram used to knock the stone walls of Masada down. I couldn't move. My heart went out to the people who must have watched in terror as the soldiers came closer and closer to their homes, who chose to end their own lives rather than be taken captive and forced into slavery.

A gust of wind blew across the ruins, sending grains of sand and small pieces of rock up our nostrils and into our eyes, stinging our bare arms and legs with needlelike pings. We began to feel thirsty as the dry heat and wind parched our throats. A small fountain provided us with fresh water, and though I'd only drunk bottled water during our tour, the need to quench my thirst was more powerful than the fear of drinking contaminated water.

I stood at the edge of the rock looking across the desert. In the distance, I saw a brown wall of sand barreling toward us. "It's the *khamseem*," a man standing next to me said. "It's an Arab word that means a hot, dry wind from the desert," he explained. "You'd better find shelter."

I had never seen anything like this before. It moved so quickly that before he uttered the last word, the sandstorm descended upon us. I ran for cover, gathering the others inside with me. Some of the elderly women coughed as the wind and dust seeped in through cracks. Soon the air was unbreatheable. After finding a room that offered more protection from the searing wind and sand, I left to check on the cable car. Much as I feared, I was told it was impossible to operate in this wind. It was far too dangerous and might blow off the cable. "How do we get down?" I asked.

The cable car operator said, "You either stay here and wait it out, or you walk down the path."

"Wait it out? How long do these storms usually last?"

"Sometimes three hours; sometimes three days," he said, nonchalantly, as if this were something that happened often.

I couldn't imagine staying on top of this isolated rock slab for three days with no food. Many of the women with me needed regular medications. Some were suffering terribly with asthma. I started down the trail to see how difficult it would be. I soon realized there was no way these women could do it. It was too steep, and the wind blew with ferocious force.

I went back up the trail and fought my way through the blinding sand, not sure if I could find them. When at last I went into the right room, I announced, "Ladies, we're in trouble, but everything will be all right."

These sweet women patted my hands. "Don't worry." Here I was, trying to comfort them, and they were comforting me instead.

I couldn't help but worry. We gathered in a circle and offered prayer. When we finished, I took them down to the cable car. "We'll wait here," I said, assuring them we'd be fine. Within a few minutes, the wind died down.

"We've enough time to take one carload down; maybe two, if we hurry," the operator announced. I told him of the women's medical needs, and they were given space on the cable car.

As I was younger and healthier, I waited for the next car down. "You'll be fine!" I shouted. I waved at them as they headed down the mountain. Once they were safe at the bottom, I relaxed.

But my fears had only begun. The operator announced that it was far too windy, and the cable car would not be coming back up. The rest of us would have to walk down the mountainside, like the goat I'd seen earlier in the day.

Nearly blinded by blowing sand, I struggled down the path. It took every ounce of energy I could muster. Between the wind and the steepness of the path, it was physically exhausting and extremely dangerous. The loose rock on the narrow path made it slippery. My legs buckled and I nearly collapsed with every step. I cried in fear when I ended up crawling on my hands and knees, along with the lizards! My throat was swollen with thirst. Finally, after two of the longest hours I've ever been forced to endure, I made it to the bottom of Masada. I staggered to the shade of a tree and collapsed. My mother, frantic with worry, came rushing to me, as did the other women who'd ridden to the bottom in the cable car. My hair was full of dirt and sand. "We were so worried about you," she said, hugging me.

"Water," I gasped. "Water."

Mom handed me her bottled water, which disappeared in one gulp. I refilled it three more times. I poured another two bottles over the top of my head, just to cool my body temperature down. It took me ten minutes with a hose to get the dirt off my face and out of my hair.

Once everyone was accounted for, we boarded the bus. I fell into my seat. Masada, in all its glory, rose majestically above us, like a stone giant. Dust and dirt swirled around it, making it difficult to see the top, or the people who were still making their way down the path. I was so grateful that the wind had died down temporarily, allowing the sick and elderly to take the cable car to safety. They'd have never made it otherwise.

The *khamseem* lasted three entire days. It didn't just cover the Judean Desert but all of Jerusalem and most of the country. That night as I lay in my clean bed, with clean sheets, clean hair, and a huge bottle of water by my side, I realized what a blessing the experience had been. I'd seen something fascinating, and yet tragic, out of Israel's past. I learned compassion for those who have in the past, or will in the future, be forced to endure the physical trials of thirst and exhaustion.

Masada, a citadel of strength and a monolith of time, will stand for eternity, a monument to those immortal souls who continue to dare to ascend its princely crown. Though time, dust, and wind have worn away the memories of its tragic history, they are renewed by each traveler who journeys to the lofty peaks of this stone giant. ☙

Picture Rocks: On Sacred Ground

Peggy Eastman

The desert will lead you to your heart where I will speak.
—Saying at Picture Rocks Retreat Center

Wordless, they reach to the sky, arms of the stately saguaro cactuses. Here, standing watch at Arizona's Picture Rocks in the desert high above Tucson, they ask nothing, expect nothing. The arms reach up in silence. The silent saguaro cactuses stand guard over a secret. The stone holds the secret: petroglyphs, symbols the Hohokam Indian tribe carved into rock 1,500 years ago. It could have been longer ago than that; no one really knows.

The stone drawings depict animals, dancing people in headdresses, and geometric designs. It is said the symbol makers, hunters or shamans, would have carved these stone drawings—running deer, leaping antelope, and bounding mountain sheep—to ensure a successful hunt and food for the tribe. According to local lore, when food was needed for the tribe, a sacred ritual was performed. It is said the picture-makers carved the likenesses of animals into the stone, and the tribe prayed and asked pardon of the ones that would be hunted and killed for food. But no one really knows.

And what of the people in headdresses? Were they tribal elders, repositories of Hohokam wisdom? And what of the geometric designs? Some are circular mazes;

where do they lead? Were they signals or mathematical signs? Did these, too, have to do with gathering food for the tribe? Or were they symbols paying wordless homage to the Great Spirit that unites all of creation? No one really knows.

Ancestors, what wisdom did you leave us in the rocks?

The Arizona Sonora Desert is the only corner of the world where the saguaro makes its natural home. It sets a sacred and hushed tone, as if these cactuses were nature's holy ones keeping the secret in stone from all but those who climb the path to find the carvings. I am here to participate in a writers' workshop held at the Redemptorist Picture Rocks Retreat Center above Tucson, but I have come more to experience the sacredness of the ancients than to write. The desert retreat center is in foothills ringed by the Tucson Mountains, bordering Saguaro National Park West. The center hunkers down on a scrub-patch of land on 120 acres of ancient sacred ground once trod by the Hohokam. At night, the stars glitter brightly like diamond chips tossed into the inverted dome of a vast inkwell. This site is one of the few that still retains the Hohokam Indian presence. They walked here. They saw the diamond-chip stars.

I walk softly where they stepped, for I know I am in the company of desert ancestors. Their presence is a faint vibration under my feet. I feel them here. I am silent, needing no words to communicate. Like the Picture Rocks. For what would I say in words?

Ancestors, what wisdom did you leave us in the rocks?

The plant and animal creatures of the desert know how to survive under extreme conditions: rainless days that scald and nights that freeze. Rocks know how to survive extremes, too. The saguaro cactuses that guard the petroglyphs are a study in patience. They do not grow their reaching arms until they are about sixty years old—late middle age for humankind. Many saguaro elders at Picture Rocks are more than 200 years old, and they have multiple, reaching arms. Until they grow arms, the saguaros stand tall and columnar, guarding their stone secret. The rocks and the saguaros tell us of solitude, of standing firm, of nonviolent resistance, of the holiness of guarding sacred secrets in stone. What message do the saguaros guard? No one really knows.

Ancestors, what message did you leave us in the rocks?

The rocks need patient guardians. The saguaros that guard the Picture Rocks carvings are a rare and wise family. They have learned to swell when they are blessed with life-giving water, to contract their ribbed bodies when water is scarce. Along with desiccation, they have learned to resist lightning strikes, freezes, and marauders. They are friends to the pollinators who help perpetuate their kind: long-nosed bats, curve-billed thrashers, and white-winged doves. Even so, less than one of every 1,000 saguaro seeds survives long enough to sprout; if it sprouts, it must grow near or under a nurse tree for shelter and succor. Gila woodpeckers, insect larvae, and desert packrats will eat fledgling saguaros if they are hungry enough. Fewer than 1 percent of nursling saguaros in the wild live longer than six weeks.

The Tohono O'odham Indians, who live in this area today, know this, and they know the power needed to guard secrets in stone, so they chant a saguaro-growing song to the "tall mothers" to encourage the slow-growing plants to grow arms and reach to the sky. Do the Tohono O'odham know how to decipher the secret language of the stone carvings? Can they read the intent of the

Hohokam carvers? No one really knows.

Ancestors, what message did you leave us in the rocks?

If they could, the rocks would tell stories of the Hohokam, ancient makers of sacred symbols, carving their soul stories into rock. If they could, the rocks would tell of a tribal smoking pipe with a much-fingered stem, and a shy, little-seen herb grown for wisdom. They would tell of bison, shag-bodied gift of the Great Spirit, and of the unity of all members of the nation's "hoop"— the world we share. I stand before the rock pictures, listening.

And now I hear without sound. If they could, the rocks would tell of the healing powers of place, how to let the desert lead a person from our time to the healing space deep within, the place where only the Spirit can speak. The place deep within is a place the Hohokam must have known well. The Tohono O'odham know that place today. To find it, one must leave the freeways and the tooting horns and the speeding cars and the buses belching smoke from the rear. To find it, one must leave the sometimes suffocating cocoon of routine and the pressing love of family for a time. To find it, one must make an acquaintance of solitude, a friend of self.

The carved rocks say nothing, but I hear. They endure the harshness of their desert home without complaint. Their mute witness humbles, pares living to an essential exchange of breath. They stand in tribute to a mystery they have kept for centuries. The praying arms of the saguaros that guard them celebrate the holiness of this silence.

Ancestors, I am listening for the message in the rocks.

I walk softly here, and I look at the leaping antelope and the dancing figures in headdresses carved into the rock, and now I am beginning to understand as well as hear. There is nothing to decipher. There is no magic in these rocks. The secret is within me. I must go deep within to find the mystery of my heart, where the Spirit will carve its wisdom.

In that silent place is peace. In that silent place is renewal. In that silent place is reorientation. In that silent place deep within is the Great Spirit that calls us all to be one. ☺

Inca Stones

Maureen Tolman Flannery

hewn smooth in gentle curves
as if the hand of a grandmother
has scooped away the parts not needed
for your ascent
or sharp and perfectly fitted to their places
as the calculations of an engineer

They speak of how devotion deep enough
cannot be blasphemed,
outlasts a crass defilement,
points a stone finger to the heavens
long after incantations have been silenced
or become the vibrant orange amid jungle green.
A reverence that defines a way of life
inspires beyond the tearing down,
melding into medium of exchange,
the breaking off of puma heads
and reconfiguring of holy stones.
When the walls have been stripped of their gold
and all the weavings torn away,
eloquent gray stones
have still the loftiest of things to say.

Holy Rocks!

Paul W. Anderson, Ph.D.

I DID HEAR A VOICE FROM INSIDE ME SAY, "DO NOT disturb any rock from its resting place. Leave all stones where you find them." I've learned many lessons from rocks and stones, but I risked my life to get this one.

It was my first visit to the Rio Grande Gorge near Taos, New Mexico.

I found a spot far above the river on the gorge rim that later became a frequented power place for me.

The Rio Grande Gorge is deep and narrow, running nearly a hundred miles north and south. From the air it looks like a long, narrow rip in the fabric of the earth. Torn out of volcanic lava flow, it continually crumbles and falls down its insides into the river bottom. At places the gorge is over 600 feet deep and never a safe place to hike. Deaths occur there every year.

I was exhilarated to be here. Across the great chasm, a red-tailed hawk challenged her two overgrown young to leave their nest hidden in a crevasse. Their family squabble was balanced by nearby swallows swooping in lazy circles, singing spring courting songs. Taos Valley sagebrush covered the mesa on either side of the Gorge with newborn green and a fragrance loaded with lilac and peppermint.

Between two boulders I found bleached bones from a small animal and accepted those as tokens of friendship. Joe and Red, spirit entities who came while meditating, whooshed me down to the Rio Grande and initiated me into the band of warriors who sweep to and fro between the steep canyon walls. The slow beat of my drum and smoke from dusting sage gave me calm. I was filled with contentment that comes from knowing purpose and a connection with everything around me.

In that frame of being, I wanted to explore the rim and gorge. A hike to the river and back would allow me to linger with all the energies present. Then I heard the voice warning me about leaving rocks alone. That was a good idea, I thought. I was the stranger in this ancient volcanic field. Rocks were everywhere, and they got here first, long before me. They certainly had squatters' rights. No problem. "Show respect and tread carefully" seemed useful advice.

Halfway down the gorge I discovered a badger's den. Its droppings amid shredded and torn scrub-pine tree limbs, as well as unmistakable footprints, easily convinced me I should keep moving. Despite my fascination and curiosity with my explorations, I walked slowly, careful to avoid dislodging stones. My pace suited me not only as a walking mediation, but it also gave me the time to see each rock's position and to pass by without challenging territorial rights.

Perhaps I was in a kind of trance or altered state, but it was not until I was stuck that I realized I could not find a passage over a precipice that dropped 200 sheer feet to the river's beachhead. I'd made several sweeps along the cliff, but there were no foot and handholds to help me climb down. At one point I thought of leaping into flight and gliding down like the buzzards circling nearby. Either my trance was not deep enough or I knew I was not evolved enough to pull off that kind of Carlos Castaneda stunt. I continued searching for a more conventional human manner of lowering myself down the cliffs.

Heat, failure, and impatience brought me to frustration. In a huff, I quickly turned to climb up a small incline and try one more time. I wanted to get back on a narrow ridge above me and continue further along the rim, hoping eventually to find a break in the solid stone wall. My pace had lost its deliberation, and I hurried. Like ball bearings, the ground beneath me rolled away, my feet slid out behind me, and I was slammed down on my front side. I had disturbed the stones.

Palms pressed to the gravelly ground and toes digging for traction, I was out of control on a slippery slope. The edge of the cliff came up fast, reaching my feet first. I felt the rocks' angry slashes at my hands. The sound of my body scraping over the sharp pebble slick was like a garbage disposal sucking water. I wondered how long it would be before my limp body was found draped over the river boulders below.

My slide stopped as suddenly as it started. I still do not know how. I lay spread eagle, stomach and palms desperately glued to millions of rock shards. Silence. No more muffled garbage disposal sounds of clothing dragged over rough soil. Every sound and sight around me returned to what it had been moments ago, as if nothing of importance had happened. I accepted this as proof I was alive, but the weakness that coursed through me left little energy and my panicked heart used that up entirely.

I was scared, dazed, and half crazed with anger at myself. How stupid could I be? Here I am, flat on my belly, by myself, dangling into this slippery gorge, a monumental display of geodesic instability. I had taken on the same feature as the gorge, only my instability was mental.

Gently I rose and stood still until some of the fear drained away. I climbed on up the incline a few feet and sat on a level outcropping. I lowered my face into my hands and felt my tears sting the bloodied cuts. It seemed I should say "Thanks" to someone, but instead I heard it again: "Do not disturb any rock from its resting place. Leave all stones right where you find them." Good idea, I thought. No problem! And with that, I was able to laugh and learn.

Whenever I return to my spot on the high rim of the Rio Grande Gorge in northern New Mexico, I feel like a stranger in someone else's garden. I quietly approach the edge as if sneaking into the middle of high mass with bishops and cardinals doing their holy rite. I sit and hope the rocks will accept me without perturbation. They seem so preoccupied. I rest and do my own rituals. I breathe in clean air purified by delicate, green mesa sagebrush. I pray. But one eye always stays cracked open to keep watch on the rocks. This is their temple, and I am a temporary intrusion on their resting place. ☺

Stone's Throw

Walter Bargen

No one said it wasn't heavy, straining
the suitcase, and the carrying. Scottish customs
wanted to see the dark object smudging
their scanner: explosives, uncut gem,
lump of uranium, mad-cow meat,
contraband cheese, but just a stone.

It was nothing that caught anyone's eye,
there on a cold, windy hilltop at Clava Cairns,
the buried bones centered in stone circles,
a moss-encrusted celestial calendar
so old they remember forward. What a primitive,

earthly souvenir to say they were there and still there,
though across the channel in Brussels. Back home
the stone closes in, his daughter breaks both her legs,
he loses his job, his wife falls seriously ill.
This is how stones are called home, through the mail
accompanied by unsigned letters of witness, of apology.

Wave Rock

Judy Ray

LOOK WEST FROM AUSTRALIA'S SOUTHWESTERN coast to apparent infinity—boundless oceans and the unfathomably huge distance to wherever the next rise of land may be. Look south from New Zealand's South Island toward Antarctica with the same sense of wonder. Follow with your eye the swoop of a royal albatross's ten-foot wingspan as the bird heads out over the oceans, perhaps not to tread on land again for a year. Thus distance binds with time.

Inland from that Australian shore lie the hills called the Darling Range, then a plateau of wheatlands, forest, and the bush. Red dirt roads intersect here and there. One has to know landmarks.

I am not traveling into the interior deserts, the dry-bone outback, yet water is on my mind even before I see a dry lake bed with a rim of dead trees, then a salt flat shining like a desert ice-rink. There is a water hole out here, I have been told, as well as a cave with ancient paintings, and a rock.

Does "water hole" make you think of a pond where animals come at sundown and leave intermingling tracks? What I find is a field of rock, maybe a five-acre field of granite with a thin, dark line across it like a scar. In that fault line lies an oval basin, small, deep, and neat. It would not be easy to locate without landmarks, either. There is water, warm and soft, though somewhat slimed and rippled with bugs. There is no sand for a filter. But it is a water hole, upheld in the aborigines' life-stories of the land.

Atop the field of rock sit boulders like Henry Moore's large *Sheep Piece* or the *Four-Part Reclining Figure,* with holes making interiors exterior. A goanna moves away from my feet, hides its head in a crevice with its body exposed. The camouflage would be perfect if I had not seen it move. If it were a matter of my survival, could I do as hunters have done for millennia—reach out and grab the goanna, hit it against the rock that protects it, bake it until charred in the ash of a fire, and eat it? Could I find the water hole again? We move so far from survival knowledge.

Farther on, the track dips down around some scrub. And there, rising about fifty feet out of the plain, is a wave, a majestic rolling wave like those in the Pacific that surfers ride. This great granite wall has the same concave curve, and a lip curling over. Yet all movement is immobile. Time is held in space. And space is held in the twenty-seven hundred million years in which this granite has heard the wind and water carving it and has become streaked with many mineral pigments.

I reclaim a word from overused vocabulary. Wave Rock is *awesome.*

The nearby cave with drawings and handprint outlines on its walls is a place of dark legend for the Aborigines. But surely the wave has uplifted and has been uplifted by whoever has been heir to its spirit song.

At the base of the rock, wind sings through pines almost the same song I heard from the ocean waves back at the coast. The human figure stands tiny against the sweeping arc. And human life is as the whisper of one raindrop. ◔

A Mystical Encounter

Mary Oberg

IN CELEBRATION OF OUR TWENTIETH WEDDING anniversary, my husband and I toured Egypt.

I remember looking at magazine pictures of the Great Sphinx and the three Great Pyramids of Cairo as a child. I wondered about those faraway places, but I never dreamed that I would get to see them in person someday.

"You're never the same after you've seen Egypt," I recalled a friend saying. She was right. I sensed that something mystical would happen around these ancient stones, but I didn't have a clue about what was in store for me.

As we cruised up the Nile, leaving Cairo behind, we also left behind the civilization we knew. We traveled on the ship by night, and by day docked and went by bus to nearby stone temple ruins.

At the Temple of Luxor, the plan was reversed. We took rooms at a hotel just a block away from the great limestone and granite ruins of the temple and ate supper before we began our exploration of the ruins. Our guide took us to the temple's far entrance.

"Look down," he said. "Now, look up." Below and above us we saw a long avenue of carved limestone sphinxes with rams' heads on the walkway to the lighted Temple of Luxor.

"Imagine that you are in the yearly procession to this temple from the Temple of Karnak, several miles away."

In the distance, the muezzin wailed the evening call to prayer from the mosque at the outer stone wall. It was easy to imagine living in ancient times, when the city of Luxor was called Thebes, the capital of the Egyptian kingdom. The pharaohs celebrated every victory and triumph with the construction of newer and grander temples to the gods, with scenes of the victory chiseled into the limestone walls. This temple—known as the Parthenon of Ancient Egypt—was considered the grandest.

As we walked among the ruins, each of us lost in our own reverie about ancient times, a temple guard approached.

"Would you like to pray in the temple?" he asked.

Startled at first, I realized that I *would* like to pray. He led me to four different temple rooms and put me in specific sitting or standing positions in each room. I felt balanced while in these rooms. I prayed in each of the rooms for a few minutes until it felt right to end my prayers.

Finally, he led me to the outer courtyard leading to the Holy of Holies. On the inner wall leading to this most sacred part of the temple, he showed me where to place my hands at shoulder height on this cool stone wall. I stood to pray with other tourists.

Placing my hands on the wall, I prayed with great intensity. Suddenly, something like electricity came out of the wall from between my hands, and hit me in the heart and chest area. I was stunned. The electric vibrations continued to course through my body as I stood, immobilized, wondering what was happening.

In those moments, I could sense my energy field being blown open. All of my chakras, the energy centers of the body, were blasted open. My feet could feel the pulsation of the earth. My hands felt magnetized. I vibrated all over my body. My chakras churned furiously.

Finally the "electricity" stopped. Dazed, I looked for the others in our group.

"I've had this strange experience," I explained to my husband and our tour guide. They listened but didn't understand what I was talking about. No one else in our group had had anything like this happen.

I floated through the rest of the Egyptian trip in an expanded state. I could feel the energy in all the other Egyptian temples and pyramids that we visited. I saw colors and saw the color of chanting in the Great Pyramid.

For the next few months after our return home, I reintegrated this expanded state into my body. As I puzzled over what happened, I realized that I was "hit in the heart" to wake me up and help me see what else I was supposed to do with my life. I felt called to learn energy healing and incorporated it into my professional life as a registered nurse at a large metropolitan medical center. I also developed a private practice in energy work for both human and animal clients.

My friend was right. Going to Egypt changed me forever. The powerful energy embodied in those ancient stones connected me with my own spiritual energy and magnified it to show me the possibilities for living my life at another level. Those possibilities were forever changed and expanded.

Since then, I've made trips to other sacred sites in the world: Arizona, New Mexico, Hawaii, and Venezuela. At all of these sites, I communed with ancient stones and ancient spirits. But none of the stones at these sacred places connected me with their energy in the way I experienced on that trip to Egypt. My soul had been waiting for that life-changing trip. ✺

Thailand Journal: Stone Temples

Denise Low

At Muayto, in Mae Hong Son,
an old temple comes apart in open air.
Edged stones return to earth. They sink
into hidden rivers of gravity. Hewn walls
roughen more each year, moss over,
become grizzled fragments.
I stand in the last stone doorway.
The opening faces east: to wind, sun,
to the slow power of mountain.
From here I could drop
into the first sky of creation.

Wall blocks from U-Mong
merge into mountain sediment.
We walk into hillside shrines—
limestone dissolved by monsoon rain,
formed into underground rooms.
There we find the shelter of raw stone.
Candlelight bevels ten thousand facets
of glittering surfaces. Fire burns
white stars in endless rock horizons.

In the Company of Stones

Patricia Lay-Dorsey

IN MICHIGAN, MARCH IS THE LONGEST MONTH of the year. Winter hangs on with tenacious, mittened fingers, and spring seems an impossible dream. On one of the grayest days, I decided to take a trip to the Four Corners of the U.S. Southwest. Four Corners refers to the area where the corners of four states—southwest Colorado, southeast Utah, northwest New Mexico, and northeast Arizona—all meet. It is a land with a mix of desert, mesas, First Nation reservations, canyons, pine forests, mountain ski resorts, petrified forests, and energy vortexes.

Five days later I was onboard Amtrak's Southwest Chief, and at 4:00 A.M. on my second day of travel I arrived in Flagstaff, Arizona. I spent that first night at a bed and breakfast, rented a car the next morning, and started driving toward Canyon de Chelly. On the way, I planned to stop overnight on the Hopi reservation. I had a hunger to be on land that was home to the first peoples to settle on this continent. I needed solitude and quiet. What better place to find it than on an endless expanse of desert under a huge sky?

I pulled into the old resort where I was to stay, hungry and tired, had an early dinner, and crashed on my bed, exhausted. I awoke about 7:00 P.M. Though I was tempted to turn over and go back to sleep, my inner voice said, *Here you are at Canyon De Chelly! Don't spend all your time in bed. Get up and explore.*

I got in my car and turned it toward the canyon. Although I didn't really know where I was headed, I soon saw I was driving on top of the canyon's ridge. I stopped the car beside what looked like a lunar landscape to my right. The sky was glowing with unearthly colors as the sun prepared to set over the desert. I got out of my car and walked toward the ridge. I carried with me the handpainted gourd rattle I'd bought from a Hopi man at the First Mesa that afternoon.

At my feet were pools of water from a recent rain; in each pool was reflected a full white moon. Here I was, standing between the golds, pinks, and purples of a sunset on my right, and the tranquil white of a full moon against a deep blue sky to my left. And what did I do? I danced. With pools of moons at my feet, I shook my rattle, chanted, and danced. All by myself.

Out of that dance, that journey into the core of the earth, that connection with the First Nations people and their sense of all life as sacred, came the entities I called Sacred Stones.

I did not plan them. Back at home, I simply picked up twenty-five stones from the Michigan shores of Lake Huron one weekend, took them home, and started drawing on them with a Rapidograph pen and black India ink. I used symbols and meanings that had flowed through me during those two days in April, two days when I felt carried along like a leaf on a spring-swollen creek. When I looked up, the Sacred Stones were lying at my side like fragments of a partially remembered dream.

For two years, I spent my time stoning on the Great Lakes that surround Michigan, gathering water-smoothed stones on which I drew suns, moons, frogs, eagles, trees, and more. I then took baskets of these hand-drawn stones—accompanied by a booklet printed with the meaning of each symbol—and sold them at community fairs and holistic conferences.

As companions to the Sacred Stones came a song, a story, photographic posters, wood-burned feathered and beaded driftwood staffs, storytelling workshops, and women's rituals. It took time, but eventually my ears grew sensitive enough to hear their whispered messages. They never steered me wrong.

I am deeply grateful for the time I've spent in the company of stones. Perhaps it is their example that has taught me to weather physical and emotional storms, to let them smooth away my rough edges, and to roll with the waves of life-as-it-is, not life-as-I-wish-it-were. ☺

Stone Refuge

Joyce Brady

WE ARRIVED AT THE COUNTY SLIGO HARBOR JUST in time to catch a small fishing boat to the island of Inishmurray, off the west coast of Ireland. After a full week of lectures, seminars, theater, and social events at the W.B. Yeats International School, Kathleen, Monika, and I skipped a poetry workshop to visit a fifth-century monastic settlement on the small island four and a half miles from the mainland. The settlement there had been built as a refuge from the world, a place to be nearer to God.

I descended a rusty ladder to the fishing boat, happy that we caught the last departure for the island. I sat on a narrow wooden seat, pulled my jacket hood tightly over my head, and waited in anticipation for the trip to begin. At first, I felt a sense of adventure, but as the boat pulled out of the harbor, apprehension crept into my awareness, quickly followed by fear. I suddenly remembered a warning: *The approach to the island is tricky because of massive stones.*

My fear grew as waves began to rock the boat. I looked around for life jackets, but there were none. The dark waters of the Atlantic surrounded our little boat like a permanent inky abyss. I wondered what was lurking below the turbulence.

The rocking motion suddenly ceased when the captain turned off the motor in what seemed to be the middle of nowhere, and coasted the vessel toward a distant mound of land. He threw bellows over one side to cushion the approach to the stony harbor. I saw massive stones jutting from the shoreline. My hands felt ice-cold, and I began to rub them together for warmth—and also as a form of private prayer. The captain turned, pointed to me, and said, "Out with you!" He steadied the boat with his outstretched arm, palm braced against the stones.

I spied a conglomeration of large moss-covered stones stretching across the water and jumped from the boat, grateful that the stones were not wet and slippery. Kathleen missed her first attempt and was pulled back to try again. Monika, the nature woman of our trio, landed easily and ran fearlessly across the stones.

I ventured across the water, one stone at a time, testing the stability of each stone, waiting for disaster to strike at any moment. When I reached a section with wide gaps between the stones, I belly-crawled, like a snake, over the water below. I was relieved when I finally reached a narrow pebbly trail leading to the settlement.

I gave my guidebook to Monika. I had no energy for written facts. I could only manage to feel my way. The sun was in full form, a blessing since all week had been drizzly—"soft days," as the Irish say.

Finally, the settlement loomed ahead, framed in shades of gray, like a black-and-white photograph with highlighted details of stone: layered walls, small enclosures, isolated clusters, and tombstones, all variations and gradations of stone and slate.

Above, white clouds hung beneath a silvery sky; below, the water was calm. As I walked around the island, my senses filled with stony formations. There was nothing else to do but be aware of the simple beauties here—sky, water birds, and stones. I was glad I had followed my urge to visit Inishmurray, despite my fears of heights and water. I was in a refuge of stone away from my busy life on the mainland, and I felt contented.

A couple of hours before departure, I met Kathleen and Monika in an isolated enclave near a few stones identified as birthing stones. There, I prepared a sacred space for tarot divination. With the Celtic cross spread as a template, we consulted the cards for insight and guidance for Monika's upcoming year. Kathleen stood on a large stone behind us facing the horizon, holding our intentions in her heart.

When a sword (symbol of the mind) challenge appeared in the reading, I realized that it also had relevance for me, because I had just experienced great mind turbulence. I had approached the island bound in fear.

The myth of King Arthur's sword, Excalibur, was a way to begin working with the sword symbol. We agreed to reread the myth and record our dreams in order to release the sword from stone (mind from fear) and subsequently return it to the Lady of the Lake (to be dissolved).

Stones and water were all around us in this setting, and they proved to be a simple key to our questions. I had been given a way to look symbolically at my fearful experience and at the same time receive guidance for Monika.

On my way back to the fishing vessel, I didn't test the large stones underfoot, because I knew I was being supported. I gave myself enough time to descend to the stony harbor and watch other visitors swimming in the blue water lagoon framed in sunlit stone. I left the island with a treasure box of gifts and memories, reflections of my life revealed among the ancient stones of Inishmurray. ◯

Nothing but Stone

Christopher Woods

They do not know why, or even what, left them in this algae-throated stream. Sunlight lapses, no longer strokes the arms of aspens. Night arrives, and the stones lie in darkness.

Water licks them, whistles sensually against their hard skin. The stones do not think of disappearing, of no longer being, or why they are wed so brief a time to water. All they know is learned from fossils pressed deep into their sturdy flesh.

I walk across them, an acrobat praying for balance. Midstream, I reach the largest, and it happens. The stream goes away, the darkening sky recedes. There is no sound or sight, only the wisdom of touch.

For a holy moment in which the world stops, there is nothing but stone. Nothing but stone anywhere in the world.

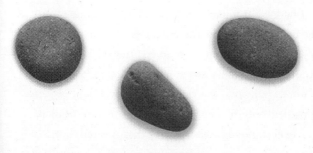

Pool Rock

Anne Heath

WHEN I WAS YOUNG, I OFTEN DAYDREAMED ABOUT a secret place. If I felt lonely or sad, or just in need of escape, I let my imagination take me deep inside a mountain. Jeweled with wildflowers, a meadow sloped gently toward a small pond where pebbles lay clearly visible on the bottom. Wind swayed the branches of a tall tree as sun warmed the ancient stone that surrounded the meadow.

Lying in imaginary grass and gazing up at a cloudless sky, I felt at one with stone and grass and tree. In that hidden world of wind and light, I belonged. Little did I imagine that one day I would discover in the outer world my dreamed-of place.

Years later, recently divorced, I found myself living in Santa Barbara, California, where I'd returned to school to earn my master's degree. Though my days were full, something intrinsic was missing. I felt disconnected, estranged—not just from my husband of fifteen years, but from an innermost part of my being.

Instinct urged me to return to the natural world, where I had spent much of my childhood. I grew up in a quiet neighborhood on the outskirts of Los Angeles. Every day after school I roamed the hills behind my house. I knew no greater joy than to follow steep trails amid pungent thickets of chaparral and sage, accompanied only by the piercing cries of a red-tailed hawk. My childhood landscape had disappeared, buried under a housing tract, but the longing was still with me. I began to look for a place in the wilderness where I could spend some solitary time. It was to be a kind of vision quest, a pilgrimage in search of—what? All I knew was that I needed to reclaim something lost.

In the belief that spiritual quests required travel to some remote place, I soon became frustrated in my search. One afternoon I went to visit an old friend. As we shared a beer on the back porch of his creek-side cottage, I told him I wanted to find a remote area to do some solo camping. I didn't speak about my deeper intention. Without hesitation, he said, "Why don't you head for the San Rafael Wilderness?"

It hadn't occurred to me that the wilderness I sought could be so near, just the other side of the sun-baked hills we could see from his porch. He spoke of a Chumash ceremonial site known as Pool Rock. Something clicked inside me; this was the place I'd been looking for.

My friend was mysteriously vague about the site's whereabouts, saying only that it would be hard to find on my own. But this was a trek I needed to make alone.

I set out early one morning, armed with backpacking gear and a topographical map. The first leg of the journey was a drive over San Marcos Pass into the Santa Ynez Valley. Spring rains had turned the valley floor into an Impressionist painting: splashes of blue and orange— lupine and poppy—on a ground of vibrant green. Figueroa Mountain, the region's tallest peak, was barely visible in the distance, wrapped in a boa of white cloud.

Beyond the lush pastures and spreading oaks of Happy Canyon, the road narrowed, then dropped into a more rugged canyon. At last the road came to an end at a small campground. I parked, heaved my pack onto my back and set off, noting with a wisp of apprehension the weathered sign at the trailhead: Lost Valley Trail.

The sun moved higher as I approached Manzana Creek. I stepped across on flat stones. Spotted trout moved upstream just below the water's surface, swaying like ghost dancers. On the other side I paused to get my bearings. A broad valley, spiked with digger pines and bordered by mountains the color of faded denim, stretched into the distance. There was no sign of human life. Three turkey vultures circled overhead, certain in their timeless purpose.

Three miles farther on, a brush-filled canyon flowed in from the left. Although the trail continued up the valley toward Fish Creek Camp I hesitated, pulled in the direction of the canyon.

The canyon trail was overgrown and faint. I followed as it snaked between high red-rock cliffs, through an elfin forest of scrub oak, manzanita, and yucca. The trail dropped into a narrow boulder-strewn draw. The air suddenly cooled. With a shiver, I quickened my pace. The unexpected chill was strange, otherworldly, as if an unseen presence had darkened my path. The canyon walls grew steeper, and the light fell to dusk.

I wondered if I'd made a mistake and taken the wrong trail. I couldn't shake the feeling that something, or someone, resented my trespass. Nonetheless, I kept going. I'd come too far to turn back now.

When the draw came to an end, the trail suddenly disappeared. I pushed back and forth through thick brush—to no avail. The trail had simply vanished.

Exhausted, I lowered myself onto the limb of a dead spruce and took a long drink of water. Was I being tested? Even the shadowy presence seemed to have deserted me. I stared blankly in the direction the trail had led, recalling my friend's warning that I wouldn't find Pool Rock without a guide.

Just then, an image appeared in my mind's eye from a dream of several nights before. In the dream, a giant bird of prey flew downward and froze against a window, wings spread wide, like the thunderbird of Native American mythology. Though I had awakened with a sense of the numinous, I did not yet know that the most coveted vision for the Chumash Indians, natives of southwestern California, was that of the dream helper, an animal spirit offering lifelong guidance and protection. The Chumash believed that without the aid of such personal spirit helpers, one could never succeed in any endeavor.

My vacant gaze fell on a shale-covered ridge, where a faint deer-track wound up the ridge's spine. With renewed energy, I scrambled up the loose shale and crawled hand and foot along the steep lower crest. Near the top, I stopped to catch my breath. About a hundred yards ahead, beyond a thicket of tall chaparral, loomed a huge hump of sandstone.

I hurried on, heart pounding in rhythm to my footfall. The chaparral formed a canopy over my head that filtered the hot sun. Sense memories of solitary childhood hours in hills like these swept through me: the dry, sour smell of sage, the sudden rush of wind, the play of light and shadow over the land. But this feeling of familiarity was mixed with another sense I couldn't name. I had entered a terrain at once known and unknown.

Suddenly the chaparral opened onto the sheer sun-washed face of an enormous monolith: Pool Rock. I stood for a long moment, looking up at the arc where stone met sky. I followed a narrow path around the base of the rock. On the far side I came to a low cave opening.

Dropping my pack, I crawled into the cool interior. Near the entrance, bits of grass and twigs lay like unfinished nests in hollowed-out pockets on the floor. The cave was still used for sacred ceremonies by modern-day descendents of the Chumash.

In one of the pockets, I discovered a small blue spiral notebook filled with notes from visitors extolling the wonders of Pool Rock. An archeologist asked that the religious purpose of the site be respected. In response, the next entry recorded an "awesome" skateboard ride in the rock's interior. I was reminded of the vulnerability of sacred sites in a world that no longer values *genus loci*, spirit of place.

As my eyes adjusted to the dim light, faded pictographs began to emerge from the cave walls. The drawings were faded, deteriorating from the passage of time and human visitors. On the nearest wall I spotted an abstract rendering of a lizard and beside it a sun symbol embellished with white dots—a striking mandala.

Depicted in a more realistic style, a large, black bird descended on its prey, wings spread in a powerful "V." I moved closer. To my astonishment, the bird was an exact replica of the image in my dream! I had plunged deep into the synchronistic world known to the shaman, the realm where outer and inner realities merge.

I left the cave and continued around the base. On the north side, the steep face gave way to a gentler angle. Indian ancestors had carved crude footholds into the rock. I picked my way upward toward the center of Pool Rock. All at once, the world of my childhood imagination lay before me.

A miniature meadow, dotted with wildflowers, sloped to a clear green pool. At the far end of the pool, the rock formed a natural picture window that opened to the bluffs beyond. Just above me, on a sandy plateau, stood a solitary pine. A soft breeze whispered through its branches. I watched as a swallow swooped from its perch in the pine, dipped with deft grace into the water, and flew off through the rock window. Ripples etched a concentric pattern across the surface of the pool, expanding toward the sandstone that embraced the tiny world.

I noticed a rounded niche in the rock above the meadow and climbed up to it. As I shed my clothes, I felt the sun's warmth on my back, the solid grain of stone under my feet. Naked, I crawled inside the niche and nestled into its protective curve. I sat perfectly still, listening, breathing. Knowing this place, at last, for the first time. ◯

Meditation

A STONE'S MEASURE OF TIME

Traveling east to west through Colorado, I spy a turn-off near the Continental Divide that opens to spectacular mountain views in every direction. I get out of the car. A footpath leads up a rocky trail, near people standing on top of a huge boulder.

It's an easy five-minute walk up the trail, with lichen-covered granite surrounding it on either side. Near the top, the trail flattens out and leads to a wide plateau of solid gray rock.

A small wooden sign is wedged into a crevice of granite: "The rock where you now stand is 1.7 billion years old."

For a moment I am breathless. I can't conceive of something that old that still exists, that I and countless others—generations and generations—have stood on, scampered over, squatted on, hunkered down on for shelter from the ever-present wind. An eternity of generations. How do you measure eternity?

We humans are not the only ones who stand on this rock at this microcosmic moment in time. A ground squirrel, one of the numerous "Colorado chipmunks," sits contentedly beside a scraggly bush growing out of another crevice. Its lifespan is even more momentary than mine. Yet it, too, makes its ephemeral mark in the span of eons.

The stone supports us all. It's hard to believe it moved and shifted with molten fury at one time in its own life, when no humans, chipmunks, or other creatures attended its birth. That was 1.7 billion years ago. Yesterday, in the eye of eternity.

Close your eyes. Spend a few moments in a centered, meditative state. Then send yourself farther and farther out into the astral plane.

See yourself standing at the beginning of time. What does it look like? What images, colors, sounds, and smells present themselves to you?

What do you notice about differences and similarities to contemporary time?

Next, experience what "eternity" feels like as you stand at the beginning of time.

Now open your eyes and choose this moment as eternity.

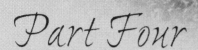

Part Four

Stone Power:
Stories of Magic and Mystery

ON THE ROAD
TED KOOSER

By the toe of my boot,
a pebble of quartz,
one drop of the earth's milk,
dirty and cold.
I held it to the light
and could almost see through it
into the grand explanation.
Put it back, something told me,
put it back and keep walking.

Mystery Stone
Maril Crabtree

KANSAS PRAIRIE SETTLERS, DIGGING THEIR SOD houses on the treeless land, dug a little deeper into a shelf of chalky limestone, left over from eons when the area lay underwater. They carved out limestone posts to string their barbed wire around. Once set in place, the limestone hardened and became weather-resistant, lasting much longer than wood. To this day, a large middle section of the state is known as Post Rock Country in honor of these fence posts that still dot the land. This same limestone was used for other things as well, from building blocks to cemetery markers. Yet nothing like the Mystery Stone has been found before nor since.

Maurice Briand, a local farmer, discovered the Mystery Stone in 1919. The land he farmed was just a few miles south of the county seat of Lincoln (pop. 1,381), in the heart of Post Rock Country. Briand, the story goes, grew tired of plowing around a flat limestone slab, which was nearly eight feet long and four feet wide. In his frustration, he and a farmhand took pick and shovel to the large slab and finally dislodged it. Beneath it, they found a terra-cotta colored stone with strange markings. It measured twelve inches long, nine inches wide, and two inches thick. On one side, inside a four-by-six-inch framed space, four lines of mysterious hieroglyphic characters were carved, with six "letters" to each line.

Briand was well-read enough to know of great archaeological discoveries such as the Rosetta Stone, which a French soldier discovered in 1799 in a small Egyptian village. The Rosetta Stone was a breakthrough key to deciphering inscriptions from Egyptian tombs.

Perhaps this is why Briand brought his strange stone to the Lincoln County Courthouse. County officials in turn donated it to the Kansas State Historical Society in the hope that learned scholars could decipher the hieroglyphic markings. There it remained, stored and undisplayed, perhaps forgotten, for more than seventy years.

Finally, in 1993, the Kansas State Historical Society returned the stone to Lincoln County, having determined that, while the stone tablet was "a worthy curiosity," the markings seemed too clean and distinct to be "of credible historical value." The Lincoln County Historical Society became the stone's new home.

Undaunted by the state's official pronouncement, the Lincoln County Historical Society board of trustees decided to protect this stone as they would any other valuable artifact. They created a special theft-proof wall display for it and placed it behind glass, where museum visitors could view it along with nineteenth-century farm implements, an old horse-drawn buggy, and an entire wall full of photos of Lincoln County High School graduates.

Although seven decades of official state pondering produced no explanation for the stone's markings, in 1999 two amateur Kansas epigraphers—brothers who had studied the stone's inscription for many years— announced startling news. They claimed that with a set of Iberian-punic and Ogam hieroglyphics as a key, they had deciphered the markings. That would make the stone's message more than 2,000 years old.

At a well-attended fund-raising dinner for the Historical Society, the brothers speculated that the stone was a sacred relic from an era long before Columbus, perhaps from a Welsh expedition or from Europeans of pre-Spanish descent.

The words seemed to be a sort of death chant, a song describing a journey from this life to the next. The brothers' translation read, "Thy Song. Strength, which powers their journey above. The one who strengthens all. Oh! Thy Song!" And the final line: "Wealth, Health, Youth."

Were the learned authorities who had rejected the Mystery Stone convinced by this new translation? No, according to newspaper accounts. Asked whether the stone could have predated Columbus, the reply was, "Basically, there's a very remote chance of that."

Has this deterred the Lincoln County Historical Society? Not in the least. In their museum—less than thirty miles from the original site of the Mystery Stone's discovery—they proudly display the artifact, along with a faded picture of Maurice Briand, in his twenties, sitting on the wooden porch of a farmhouse. Two small barefoot children stand beside him, while his wife peers from behind a screened door, holding a baby. Next to the photograph, framed newspaper clippings dating from the time of the original find give all the details.

Briand died in 1978, and his descendants profess to have no direct knowledge of whether the stone is authentic. Did some Kansas skeptic or hoax perpetrator create the stone and bury it, intending to stump the experts or gain wealth and fame? How long did the carefully carved stone lie under that limestone slab? A year? A hundred years? Two thousand years? Like the

Shroud of Turin, the stone remains cloaked in mystery, perhaps awaiting further technological breakthroughs to determine its final place in history.

Regardless of whether the stone is a hoax or an ancient sacred relic, the historical fact remains that it was found on Lincoln County land by a Lincoln County farmer—and therefore is worthy of a place in the Lincoln County State Historical Museum. If you're driving through Kansas, you might want to stop, take a look, and decide for yourself. ☺

Little Bits of Magic

Michelle Auerbach

WHEN I WAS TEN OR ELEVEN, I THOUGHT OF MYSELF as a sorceress. I did consent to masquerade as a sixth-grader at Ludlow Elementary School, but even there, my best friend Matt and I always knew we were condescending to look like plain old kids. Matt was a wizard and knew as many spells as I did.

Matt had to practice the violin, and unless we unleashed our powers, nothing could fix that. Violin practice took time, and though I read under the piano while he practiced, it felt as though the violin kept us apart. The division felt deeply unfair. While we were motivated to do something about this problem the only way we could—that is, with our magic powers—it felt wrong to use magic on our parents.

This led us to wrestle with the ethics of our situation.

When and where do you use magic, and who do you let in on your secret?

We came to this conclusion: magic is sacred and private, something to be saved for the stream at the golf course, where we became our true mythic selves, and nowhere else.

We developed a code of writing in runes so that we could communicate about the mythic world while we skimmed through the school day. We never talked on the phone. We weren't completely comfortable at school and definitely not at home.

The only safe place for us was the creek.

Matt and I lay on our stomachs for hours trying to levitate stones. We found a spot by the creek at the golf course near my house, and we searched for the perfect stone of the right size and heft. Too big, and levitation would be impossible; too small, and the act would be too easy. A flattish shape was best, so that you could get a better mental grip on the stone.

"Did you see that one? Did it almost move?" he asked.

"No, it might have, I didn't see." I said.

What must have happened, we consoled ourselves, was that we had lost the power stone. The key to teaching us our magical powers was in this stone. Without it, we were bound by the rules of this earthly plane.

That stinks, we thought.

The search started for the power stone.

We reread our favorite books, we went to the library (almost as safe as the stream), and looked in every text we could find. We found no reference to power stones, but I noticed that there were not many female sorcerers.

At home, my mom was getting divorced. From her second husband. No one else had parents who were divorced—even once, let alone twice. I thought better of mentioning this development to my friends at school. I was too ashamed to tell Matt.

I am sure their parents knew. Everyone knew. It was a small and gossipy town, and my mom was having an especially juicy divorce.

One night, just after my stepdad had moved out, I found myself curled up in a ball inside the bottom of my cube nightstand, shaking. I called Matt when I failed to get him telepathically. He was going on and on, as only an eleven-year-old boy can, about the makeup of the power stone.

"Gordon moved out." I said.

"Oh," he said. At least he shut up.

"I'm scared," I said.

"Oh."

"Do you hate me?" I asked.

"What?"

And nothing changed. He never mentioned it again. I still felt that if anyone knew about my mom, they would be disgusted. We went on reading Tolkien, the Mabinogion, the Kalevala, Hesiod's *Theogony*, Lloyd Alexander, geology textbooks—anything, hoping for some sign about the stone.

One day something happened. We were at the creek, and I moved a rock. A small one. Almost too small. A thumbnail-sized gray stone, nondescript except for its shape, which looked like a heart.

"You really moved that one," Matt said, letting me know he knew. We had been leading each other on before, but this time it was for real.

"I know. I felt it. I felt something leap out of the sky, through my head, and make the stone move."

I gave him the stone to examine. He held it but didn't try to move it. It was mine. He handed it back to me, and I put it in my pocket. I always wore jeans, never skirts. In my life as a sorceress, I would have gowns, but on this plane I was stuck in Levis.

I wanted to give Matt the stone. He needed to learn to move rocks too. It was part of being a journeyman sorcerer. But he didn't ask for it, and I didn't mention it. I mumbled something and ran home.

Matt, bless him, never mentioned the power stone

again. I could never have given it up. I carried it everywhere. It protected me from the stares of my classmates and the shame I felt when I saw my mom leave the house on a date. It was the power stone we had searched for—that was for sure.

I still have that stone in a tiny jar. A jar my mom's third husband brought me from India, the one I call "Dad," who gave me away at my wedding.

The only feeling I have ever had that was anything close to the feeling of moving that rock came during childbirth—that I was *meant* to do this, I could not think about it, and all I needed to do was get out of the way. What reached through me to move that stone was exactly what moved through me to give birth to three children: love.

I disagree with the ethics of magic that Matt and I constructed twenty-odd years ago. Magic is not secret, nor is it private, nor is it to be used sparingly. Stones are little bits of magic to be used when magic is what you need. The kind of magic I found in the power stone is waiting to be found by anyone who wants it, just strewn around on creek banks—and a good thing, too. ☯

A Stone in the Road

Ted T. Cable

Let us, then, be up and doing,
With a heart for any fate
—Henry Wadsworth Longfellow

FIGHTING THE GODS IS FUTILE. ROAD-BUILDERS came to this conclusion on the outskirts of Larabanga, a dusty and ancient village in northern Ghana. In the 1950s, as construction workers cleared the route for a new road to town, they encountered a boulder blocking the way. The red-brown stone, flat and oval, measured about two feet thick and five across. It was much too heavy for the men to pick up with their hands and carry off to the side. Using ropes and levers to lift the stone, and with all the strength they could muster, the workers wrestled the stone off to the side of the road.

The next morning, to the amazement of the stunned crew, the stone was back in its original location. Once again, the men struggled and strained to move the stone off to the side. They then went on with their roadwork, wondering who had played this trick on them.

As the next dawn broke over the savanna, the workers again found the stone in the middle of the roadway. Blinded by a degree of persistence bordering on stubbornness, the workers once again fought the stone over to the side of the road. Their sense of wonder had turned to frustration and anger.

Another sunrise brought another astonishing discovery. The stone was back in its original location for a third time. Finally, the workers concluded that this was indeed a special stone, and the gods were moving it back to its original sacred place each night. Instead of moving the stone for a fourth time, the humbled road builders decided to leave the rock in its sacred place and build the road around it.

Today the stone is perched upon a rock pedestal. The road makes a direct approach to the stone then curves sharply around it. Tourists travel to Larabanga to see a picturesque, centuries-old whitewashed mud mosque. Invariably, they also make a point of seeing the sacred stone that refused to be moved. Some visitors leave offerings of coins or food at its base. Others lay hands on it and believe they can feel its power.

I visited the stone while leading college students on a trip through West Africa. The visit to the stone affected each student differently, but they all recognized that they were viewing a special place, a sacred site.

As for me, burdened with plans, programs, itineraries, and responsibilities, I took the lesson of the stone with me over the remaining 1,000 miles, which were marked by bus breakdowns, dangerous encounters with poachers and wild animals, dust storms, detours, and delays.

Like the road-builders, rather than fighting fate, I decided to be willing to change course. I chose to go around obstacles rather than futilely fighting the gods. The sacred stone of Larabanga taught me that as I journey through life, rather than dreading detours, I should delight in deviations. ◎

Hearing Stones Speak
Susan Elizabeth Hale

To UNDERSTAND THE LANGUAGE OF STONES, TO HEAR them speak, one needs to hear rock bands of granite and slate, to rock around the clock into timeless time, to remember a different way of knowing.

While teaching a weeklong workshop at a retreat center in New Mexico, I asked students to find a rock that spoke to them. I asked them to hold this rock in their hands, listen to the music inside the stone, and sing along with it. Some could not make this leap. One woman looked at me as if I were crazy and said, "I have a hard time believing this rock is really alive." To the Western industrialized mind, rocks are dead objects.

If we don't know how to listen to ourselves and to each other, how can we listen to stones? Thomas Berry, noted philosopher and cultural historian, and other ecological thinkers have noted that we have forgotten how to communicate with other forms of life. We have long since lost a sense of kinship with anything other than, our own kind, at best.

This woman did not recognize a kinship with stones. But later in the week, after a hike to Box Canyon and time alone in the salmon-colored sandstone mesas, she began to feel a pulse inside her stone. She had created a relationship with the rock in her hand and with the rock within. She had found her sound response and sang with the rock and to the rock beings she saw in the mesas along the trail. It had taken only a week for her to remember that she, too, was a voice of the earth.

At the end of the week, I led a ritual at Echo Amphitheater in which we sent our names, intentions, and sounds into its mouth for them to be echoed out into the world.

I went to the amphitheater with photographer and architect Marc Schevene. Marc and I first met in a gallery in the tiny town of Paonia, Colorado. He pulled his black portfolio out from underneath a counter and said, "I want to show you something." His portfolio was full of cobalt-blue-and-white photographs of the world within stone. In the photos I saw rock devas, guardians, holograms, star-streaked shamans, totems carved in time, ceremonial chambers, a chalice of light, doorways into the secrets within stones.

"I know how to sing these," I said, surprising even myself. I breathed in, not only the images I saw, but the voices I heard: voices of water and granite; the sound of starlight etched onto rock faces; echoes of ocean; psalms of shadow and light; rocky tongues unleashed. I followed the blueprint of the stones and traced them in the air with my voice. Then silence. Marc said, "I've been waiting for you."

Over time, the stones have taken Marc and me to many places. We sang in a vapor cave, listening to the sound of our voices within stone. We prayed inside a sandstone shrine. We created a ritual performance, called it *Allegorian Chants*, and took it to Colorado, Arizona, and New Mexico. The photos were projected onto white silk. I sang and read poetry from behind the silk.

Wrinkled rock
veined with age
who would know the light
that dances in your heart

To look at you, old one,
I see solid weight
still
unmoved
stone face

Yet in your body
stars leap
rivers run
fires burn
oceans churn
air drifts
through you all time
sifts

As I sang the blue-rock spirits, I felt as if I had penetrated the white silk veil and merged into the world of stone beings. The hard surface of the rocks became silken, like a watery mirror. Like Alice, I stepped through the mirror and saw the rock face as my face, the echo of stone as my voice. One of the witnesses of *Allegorian Chants* said, "I became part of the art. It evoked the deepest place in me. I had an ageless response. It was like being born a billion years ago, going within stone to the deepest void for discovery."

Marc also takes pictures of nature spirits. He stalks them in the wilderness and in his travels. He writes, "They are shy, my subjects, but also a little vain and secretly exhibitionistic: these elementals and devas, these *djads* and driads, these sylvan dances of living waters, these watching and waiting ancient earth faces, the world of fairy and the deep heart of stone, the secret forest places—this is my home. The dancers in the moonlight, the singers of the dawn, the people of the pillow, the keepers of the song."

Now we arrive again at the Echo Amphitheater in northern New Mexico. Wet sheets of rain fall over the rocks, coaxing the rock people out of their hiding places. There they are: a large-breasted skirted woman; a face with a juniper nose; wise, patient stone faces coming to look at these two people standing under a tin-roofed shelter in the middle of a rainstorm. The canyon echoes with thunder. Lightning flashes around us.

Earlier, the amphitheater was crowded. Tourists in shorts and hats "yoo-hooed," and "helloed" into the rocks, then took their voices back. A few tried coyote howls. A man clapped briefly. A group of kids made the rocks rumble like a horror movie. Their shrieks and growls mingled together. Some European women nearby rolled their eyes. "They must be from New York City," they said. The sounds of the kids were ferocious. Their voices together created one huge rock howl; the amphitheater became a giant groaning mouth.

But now all these voices are gone, and we're alone in the rain waiting for the stone people to show themselves. One at a time they come out, curiously staring back, or, like a shy violet, showing themselves briefly before disappearing as the light changes. Some wink at us. Some stand silent. Some have rain-and-thunder voices. Some echo the white-breasted swift that darts in and out of crevices. Each has a million-year-old story to tell. Yet they also seem to ask, "What do you know? What have you seen? Tell us what's happening down the road. Why do you rush off so quickly? Stay awhile. Sing to us."

> *Amazing grace . . . grace*
> *How sweet the sound . . . the sound*

The rock faces sing back to me as I teach them this 200-year-old human song. This is what we do as humans. We put our thoughts and feelings into words. And sometimes the words are true and lasting. We sing these words during times of awe and reverence, in places like this, when regular words fail and we remember a familiar song that expresses what we can't say with our own words.

Sometimes I offer my voice as a reflector of the beauty around me. I offer wordless tones that are both my human feelings of awe and love and a mirroring of what I sense is here: surface, color, texture; the individual grains that make up whole rocks; molecules that dance inside still surfaces; space and light breathed by stones. I hear these sounds and echo them back, so the rocks can hear themselves, so that I can say, "I hear you. You are beautiful."

Perhaps the rocks don't hear me in this human way. Humans have always anthropomorphized the natural world as a way to try to comprehend something that the logical mind can never truly comprehend. But something is given and something received: breath, song, love, vision.

We need each other. Humans and stones. Children and canyons. Men and caves. Women and forests. Lovers and stars. We are all together in nature's circle, part of the same dance. And if we stay a little longer in the rain, extend our breath a little longer in song, maybe something in our human nature will be stirred, some ancient way of knowing will be remembered. Mother Nature assures us that we are not alone, that there are rock people waiting to peek around a boulder to say "Hello." ☙

Note: This story is an excerpt from the author's forthcoming book, Sacred Space—Sacred Sound.

Stone Lullaby

Maril Crabtree

Go and find some part of nature,
a friend said. *Spend an hour with it.*
Let it speak to you.

I am a person of the air. I search
the skies, catch clouds that curl
into each other until
they disappear against the mountain's face.
I have passion for the water,
watch the roar and rush of restless drops
pound the mountain's feet.
I am not a person of the earth.
I journey last to a granite boulder rising
from the mountain's ribs.
I scramble up its knobby flanks
and find a place on top to lie
spread-eagle, belly down, ear to stone.

I'm here, I whisper. *I'm listening.*
In the stone's warm silence
I hear *welcome*.
My body nestles into its crevices
like a newborn into its mother's cream.
Stone flutes whistle from the depths,
carve a song like no other
in my softened flesh.
When you know me,
you know the first one,
my stone sings, *and also the last.*
When you know me, you know
all there is.
And it begins again with you.

A Sacred Gemstone of Ancient Egypt

Janet Cunningham, Ph.D.

IN THE EARLY 1980S, I HAD THE OPPORTUNITY TO sit in the presence of Twylah Nitsch, author of *Language of the Stones*. Grandmother Twylah, who is honored as a Seneca elder, lives on the Cattaraugus Indian Reservation.

That evening, Grandmother Twylah spoke about "the language of the stones," and I learned about how Native Americans honored all of the many varieties of stones for their stories, their healing capacity, and their messages. I look back on that time as my first awakening to the healing properties, qualities, and messages stones can bring us. It wasn't until almost ten years later that I had an uncanny experience that spoke directly to me about the power of stones.

I had offered to be the subject in a hypnosis session for my friend Suzin, who was taking training to learn regression therapy, which is also my profession. Regression therapy—including past lives—is becoming recognized as a powerful healing modality. At the same time, even though I've done several thousand individual regressions into what we call "past lives," I don't claim to know what these memories are. They could be actual memories of one soul's experience, incarnation after incarnation. Alternatively, they could be metaphors from the unconscious, or insight gained from tapping into what

Carl Jung called "the collective unconscious." What I do know is that we all have memories of other times and other places. Perhaps most important, those memories are—absolutely—affecting us now, in the present.

In my regression, my unconscious mind took me back to ancient Egypt.

I was a young woman studying "that of the mind" in the temple. I remembered particular techniques that I practiced over and over to help expand my consciousness. I became adept at feeling and sensing energies outside of my body-mind system.

In what seemed to be an important ritual of accomplishment, my master-teacher put a woven gold collar around my neck, a large and stunning amethyst stone at its center. The adornment seemed to symbolize the high level that I had reached. I was aware that the beautiful stone hung directly over my heart.

As Suzin guided me in the regression, my next practice was to send my mind outside the temple walls. Until that moment I had been moving along rather matter-of-factly and in control. Suddenly, my mind felt enormous pain from the people outside the temple walls. In the regression, I put my hand over my heart and had to take deep breaths as tears poured down my face.

Still in a trance state, with eyes closed, when I was able I expressed my inner memories to the others sitting in the room around me in present time:

The people . . . there is such pain! The anger, the sadness . . . they pull each other down . . . they affect each other . . . their emotions connect and they pull each other down. They don't know how to lift [their consciousness].

Suddenly, from a higher awareness I shared, in a soft voice, the greatest realization of all.

Our consciousness can never be lifted as long as we feel separated from those in bondage to their minds and emotions. The temple walls do not separate us. As long as those outside the walls do not understand, the consciousness on the planet cannot lift.

Those of us who had been taught within the temples (and I spoke about all temples and spiritual truths of all cultures) had a responsibility to share the wisdom.

"We are not separate," I said softly. "Until *all* of humanity can lift, none is free."

That lifetime ended abruptly and unexpectedly. At my death, I felt my spirit leave my body. I sensed great sadness at the lack of understanding about the power of mind and spirit.

When Suzin brought me back to a state of present awareness, I realized that the people in the room were wiping their eyes with tissues as they sat in stunned silence.

One woman expressed her perception. "Janet, I feel that you need to get an amethyst stone and wear it over your heart." I recalled that a friend had given me a chain of small amethysts about two years ago. It could either be worn long or shortened with a clasp and worn around the neck. I realized that I had *only* worn the amethyst necklace at my neck . . . carefully avoiding having the stones fall over my heart. Is it possible that I had unconsciously kept from wearing the stones over my heart? When I admitted this to the group, Suzin exclaimed, "You definitely need a nice amethyst; we'll shop for one together."

Over the next several months, Suzin and I, individually, looked for an attractive amethyst necklace, with no success. It surprised me, because Suzin owned a large New Age store and had constant access to a vast array of beautiful jewelry.

Months later, Suzin and I left for a cruise to the Caribbean, on which she had arranged a speaking engagement for me. When the ship docked at one of the ports, she and I casually wandered into a store to look at jewelry. Suzin was making purchases for her store, and it was fun to watch her as she sought out high-quality and one-of-a-kind pieces.

I wandered to the other side of the store, and it was if my energy field moved me directly to a beautiful amethyst pendant, set in gold. My spirit seemed to say, *this is it—this is the one for you!* While I struggled with trying to justify the cost, I knew that I fully intended to buy it.

When Suzin saw it, her eyes brightened with excitement. She approved of the style and quality, but when she held it up to the light her mouth dropped open in astonishment. She looked at me and blurted out something that I had not seen.

"Janet, it has two pyramids in it!"

The unusual circumstances around the memories of ancient Egypt, and being guided to an amethyst stone with two pyramids, went beyond my logical mind's ability to grasp and understand.

More seemingly unrelated events continued to evolve. I received an invitation to be a co-leader for health-care professionals who remembered Egyptian past lives. I finally walked in the marvelous land of Egypt and felt as if I had come home. I began researching and studying ancient Egyptian spiritual beliefs in energy bodies. Over and over, I received guidance that my next book would be about ancient Egypt. When the amethyst came into my life, I could never have known that, nearly nine years later, I would write a book related to ancient Egyptian spiritual beliefs and their wisdom teachings. ◯

Note: Excerpts from the regression described above are from Janet's book, coauthored with Tianna Conte-Dubs, Love's Fire: Initiation into the 21st Century.

Jacob's Pillow

A Hebrew folktale retold by Robert Rubinstein

There are people with hearts of stone—
and stones with the hearts of people.
—Popular Israeli folksong

JACOB, THE SON OF ISAAC, SET OUT FROM Beersheba to walk the hot, dusty road to Haran. The rocks and stones that lay all along the roadside talked about Jacob's journey.

"Jacob goes to Haran to find a bride," said one large, heart-shaped rock.

"I have seen many beautiful women pass this way on the road to Haran," announced a gray boulder.

A small, pure-white pebble rolled by the rocks listening to what they said. "But Jacob does not search for just a beautiful woman, not any beautiful woman. He searches for a wife, one who has wisdom and understanding. He looks for a woman who will become the mother of their children, and who will teach and raise their children well," said the pebble. "It is told that Jacob will be the father of a great people."

The other stones and rocks heard the words of the white pebble. They nodded—and said no more.

The sun beat down ferociously. Some rocks merely reflected the heat back into the air; others calmly absorbed the sun's rays.

But Jacob felt the full, withering force of the intense heat. His face dripped with sweat. He was so tired, so thirsty, that he just wanted to sit down in the middle of the road. He didn't want to take another step. But, if he sat down, even for a moment, he would not be able to stand again, and the sun would bake him alive.

The stones and rocks and boulders watched Jacob, fearing he would fall at any second.

The white pebble sang out into the hot afternoon stillness, "Move on, Jacob. You must walk, Jacob. Your bride awaits you."

Two rocks that sparkled like diamonds chanted together, "Do not lie down. Do not lie down. Move on."

Jacob stopped to wipe the stinging sweat from his eyes. He sipped some cool water from a skin bag he carried at his side. Suddenly, the skin bag slipped from his hands. The water poured out on to the dusty road. The water made a dark splotch on the road. Then the sun's heat evaporated it, and the water disappeared. And Jacob's thirst increased. He stumbled and fell to his knees.

"Rise, Jacob. You must rise. See the sun as the moon. Feel the moon's evening coolness," sang the white pebble. "Keep to the road, Jacob. Stand and walk. Move on."

Jacob slowly struggled to his feet. He lurched forward. He seemed to have heard the voices of the stones and rocks, the singing voice of the white pebble as it followed Jacob on his journey. His legs shook. His arms felt so heavy now that he could no longer lift a hand to wipe his forehead. The white pebble rolled along the road, keeping pace with Jacob.

"Hear of a beautiful lamb, Jacob. She tends the flocks. She waits for you."

As the sun began to set, the coolness of evening spread out over the land. The air carried moisture and comfort to Jacob's lips. He stopped to rest for the night and set about searching for stones that might be his pillow.

"I am firm, Jacob. Please use me as your pillow," said a large, blue-colored rock.

"Choose me—choose me, great Jacob. I am smooth and flat. Your head will rest comfortably on me." And the flat sandstone tried to stretch itself toward Jacob's fingers.

"I am like a cradle. Your head will not slip from me in the night, Jacob. I will hold you safely and easily," hummed a sun-bleached rock. Many of the pebbles and smaller stones along the road felt sad that they were too small to serve as Jacob's pillow.

But the white pebble rolled along the road near them and said, "You will all serve. The small and the large, the flat and the round, the firm and the soft. You will serve. Wait and see."

In the dark of the wilderness night, a lightening bolt flashed. It struck the road near Jacob's resting place. Through some miracle, as the lightning flashed down and the thunder rolled above, the blue-colored rock, the flat sandstone, the sun-bleached rock, and many of the smaller stones fused together to form the wonderful rock that served as Jacob's pillow for that night. In the very center of this rock lay the white pebble.

Jacob lay down and slept with his head cradled gently, safely, firmly by the rock. He dreamed a wondrous dream that night—and climbed a ladder to Heaven.

And when Jacob awoke the next morning, he stood the rock that had been his pillow on end. He poured oil over the rock, making the rock holy—and making this place where the rock stood a holy place.

And Jacob called this place Beth-el—"The House of God." ◯

Note: This story is excerpted from the author's CD, Strange Tales from Biblical Times.

Smooth Stones

Thomas Zvi Wilson

. . . and [David] chose him five smooth stones
out of the brook, and put them
in a shepherd's bag. . . And David put his
hand in his bag, and took thence a stone,
and slang it . . .
—1 Samuel 17:40, 17:49

Earth's swollen belly erupts stones frequently.
I've never tripped over one that wasn't old.
Do they calculate their age without a watch,
count each sun's rising and disguised hiding?

Do stones beat a heart, treasure a soul?
They often camouflage in earth or water,
bask on hillsides, or are shaped by currents,
and occasionally by human hands

that fondle and form stones to hang
round necks or add to pockets' weights,
hard eggs laid by devils or saints,
or talismans to depend upon and name.

Abreast a village church, checkerboards
of smooth stones can be an endless walk
from end to end, or on Mount Moriah each
stone climbed the Wailing Wall, never to fall.

Look and You Shall Receive

Sande Hart

ALTHOUGH A HEART-SHAPED DIAMOND IS SPECIAL, I discovered that a heart-shaped rock, found at the river by my ten-year-old son, held much more value.

For the last decade, we have been taking family river trips. We take our boat to Lake Mojave where the scenery has not changed for tens of thousands of years. The majestic towering rocks surrounding the lake disappear dramatically into the deep water. As I look at the mountain ranges, I can fantasize all the secrets they seem to keep. Lake Mojave is a spiritual place where I can regroup with God and my kids can water-ski.

One summer, as I sat secluded in a cove some eight miles away from other sun worshippers, my son came from around a bush with a heart-shaped rock that he had found as he was looking for his wayward Frisbee. I was amazed at what a perfect heart it was, but I was even more impressed that he thought of me when he saw it and brought it to me.

We brought the rock home and placed it on our bookshelf. The shelf also holds a humanitarian award, my husband's high school soccer most valuable player award, and a few other special mementos. Whenever anyone stops to look at that shelf, it's always the heart-shaped rock they notice. To me, the manmade awards were special, but this was a "God-made" award brought to me by my son.

Today we have a large collection of heart-shaped rocks creatively perched on the bookshelf. Some are in front of family pictures, some lean on others so as to show off their shapes. Some of the bigger rocks sit on our front porch, welcoming guests to our home. My sister recently brought me back a heart-shaped stone that she found near Yellowstone National Forest. I keep that stone in my wallet, and it reminds me of her every time I see it.

Rocks are there for us to find what we want from their magic. When we come from the heart, even greater magic happens. I also believe that when we know what we are looking for, it is always there for us to find. We just have to be willing to look for it. ☺

Riker's Stone

Liz Palika

IT HAD BEEN A BAD DAY. CLIENTS HAD BEEN FUSSY, demanding, and short-tempered, and I could feel myself moving in the same direction. To try to short-circuit the bad mood, I called to my dogs and we went out for a walk.

As we walked, I consciously took in deep breaths of fresh air, clearing and cleaning my lungs. I made it a point, too, to look around me, to appreciate the new green leaves on the trees and the spring flowers. I also watched my dogs. I take pleasure from their enjoyment of the world around us, and they make me see things I might not have otherwise seen.

When we reached the riverbed, I took the dogs off their leashes and let them run. They ran, played, and sniffed, and I tried to think of positive things.

Unfortunately, my mind kept drifting back to a few difficult customers. Every time I felt myself begin to relax, I remembered Mr. Simpson's excuses, along with Mrs. Harris's outrageous demands for more of my time and assistance. I love working with people and helping them, but people themselves can also make this very difficult to do.

As I walked and tried not to think, I noticed Riker, my youngest Australian Shepherd, sniffing in the rocks along the side of the riverbed. He appeared to be searching for something. I called him, asking him to come to me. He looked up at me, made eye contact, and then went back to sniffing the rocks. Riker never ignores me, so I walked over to see what he was searching for.

When I was halfway there, he picked something up, rolled it around in his mouth, and trotted toward me. When he got to me, he stood in front of me, again making eye contact. I held out my hand. He dropped a rock in my hand. A rock?! Riker doesn't play with rocks!

Then I realized he had given me: a well-worn, water-polished piece of rose quartz, covered in dog drool but still eye-catching. About the size of a cherry tomato, it was the pink of an early-evening sunset. It was warm from Riker's mouth but got warmer in my hand as I held it.

My knees were weak, and I had to sit on the ground to hug my dog. He crawled into my lap and licked my face.

Rose quartz is a powerful sacred stone. Even small pieces are good for healing, but most importantly, rose quartz can calm and ease mental turmoil.

Had Riker felt my distress? Did he realize that I really hate it when clients affect me so strongly? Did he sense the approaching bad mood and search out this stone to help me release it? When he rolled the stone around in his mouth, was he testing it to see if it had power? I would like to believe he was and is so perceptive.

Today, Riker is still my best friend, and we both still have that lovely sacred rose quartz. Riker and the stone are the best medicine for me. ☯

On the Beach, Walking Bella

Hannah Wilson

Like Beckett's Molloy, I used to keep only one stone in
  my pocket
not to suck but to mound in the bowl with others
I culled from this beach, one to a walk.
Each time another drew me down I took out the first,
forced the choice, right hand or left.
What if we all came home with pocketfuls?
How much blankness could the ocean tolerate,
nothing left to scoop and scrape and toss
back, polished, more or less jagged, rock and pebble and
  sand?

But today in a sudden calm, the tide lowering,
temptations pock the beach: a glistening wedge of black,
lined, I want to believe, by an embedded leaf;
a common knobbly red; an amber locket-sized
oval with needled ebony veins; a clouded blue
with wash of ocher; striated grays; rusted sandstones—
and I cannot let any of them go,
my right-hand pocket now heavier than the left,
already crammed with dog biscuits and my wool hat.

Bella once thought each bend of my back meant
I was picking up something for her to chase. Now

(continued on next page)

she hoists one arthritic leg after another, not even
  pretending
to keep up. The dog knows her own way back.
She stands in the shallows looking out to where
she once swam with gulls, her neck arched, her
  nose high
as if measuring how far she has to swim
to reach whatever she scents there, tumbling beyond
waves, beyond light.

My Crystal Ball

Roberta Gordon Silver

ON MY BEDSIDE TABLE, A ROUND GOLF-BALL–SIZED crystal sits cupped in a plaster mold of miniaturized hands. The clear, electronic quartz orb sparkles in the morning sunlight, catching my eye when I awaken.

When I received the crystal as a gift, it came with a book on metaphysical properties of minerals. I learned that quartz crystals amplify energy in positive ways. The holder may send positive thoughts to others or meditate, becoming more intuitive, calm, and balanced. In addition, these crystals may be used in healing. I learned, for example, that they could be used to reduce fever or to discharge pain by drawing away the heat of inflammation.

The stone had value to me mainly as an object of beauty. Aside from its twinkling appeal, I liked the feel of the smooth ball in my hand and against my cheek. I enjoyed the crystal for its sensual attributes but didn't use it for healing. Then something happened to change my mind about its power.

I had retired from teaching in California, rented my condo, and moved back to the Midwest to be near my family. Without warning, however, my tenants moved out, and I was faced with the possibility of financial disaster. I decided the best thing to do would be to live in the condo and work there until it sold.

With much anxiety, I loaded my car with all the possessions I'd need. I took only the bare essentials to furnish my temporary residence. I'd be camping in style with an air mattress, card table, lamp, folding chairs, and some cooking utensils.

To avoid the worst weather, I chose a southern route. The highway passed through Flagstaff, Arizona, only a short distance north of Sedona. People claimed that the energy or magnetism there centered them, and for years I'd yearned to experience its power. On impulse, I turned south.

It had snowed during the night, leaving a blanket of white on the evergreens lining the road. Sunlight slanted between the pines as if through stained glass. The exquisite winter landscape astounded me. The highway wound its way through a shimmering wonderland into stark canyons of red rock.

I took a jeep tour into the midst of jagged rocks and eroded monoliths. I felt awed and excited. At the end of the adventure, I visited a store that sold crystals and books on Sedona's vortices, places of sacred power to many. I heard talk of a palpable energy emitted from the special formations and couldn't wait to get close to them.

I drove to two sites that evening, and I saw what the setting sun did to the red mountains. A gentle paintbrush gilded the ridges with copper and gold. In reverence, my spirits soared.

The next morning I hiked to the base of one of the formations. I rested under a lone tree on terraced rock and soaked up the rare atmosphere. A feeling of utter peacefulness flowed through me. I napped for a while in the dappled shade. When I opened my eyes again, I surveyed the panoramic vision of azure sky and puffy clouds nestling on mountain peaks. I experienced no stress or worry. Everything was as it should be.

In this happy state, I reached into my pocket and removed my crystal ball. I placed it in my left hand, palm open, and held it out to the sun. Instantly, a beam of light, like a laser, struck the orb. Rays shot out at the point of entry, like an explosion of glittering light. Before my awed gaze, the beam penetrated the crystal and pierced deep into my hand with a sharp pain.

Stunned, I withdrew my hand from the sun. The hurt stopped. What an interesting development! That had never happened before. Experimenting, I put the ball into my other hand and held it in the light. Again, a bright beam entered the crystal, with rays shooting daggers in every direction. An even sharper pain stabbed my hand, and I quickly slipped the crystal back into my pocket.

Wrapping my arms around my knees, I stared at the craggy mountains before me and thought about what had happened. The power of the vortex must have charged my crystal. As I sat there, I could feel a sense of confidence and serenity growing inside me, replacing any negative thoughts or worries. I felt eager to take control of my life.

In California, I tested the sun's effect on my crystal again, to see if the hand pain occurred only in Sedona. Although the sun made the crystal shine beautifully, my hand didn't hurt. I felt certain that the vortex had a special effect. It turned my crystal into a healing stone and brought me good fortune, as well as good health. I had more job offers than I could accept, and my condo sold in a short time. A few months later, I returned to the Midwest.

Since the crystal became charged with power in Sedona, it has changed from an object of beauty to a sacred stone, capable of assisting the body's natural healing abilities. When my grandson had a fever, I held it against his back, and his temperature returned to normal. When I have occasional aches and pains, I hold the crystal against the affected area and the pain disappears.

Recently, a construction worker helped in a project at my house. One day he reported to work bent over, grimacing in agony from cramped muscles.

"I might be able to help you," I said. I retrieved my crystal and asked him to sit down.

Reluctantly, he obeyed. "I don't know," he said. "Touching or massage usually makes it worse."

"Don't worry," I assured him. "I won't press hard. I'll just hold it next to your skin."

Gently, I placed the crystal next to the place he indicated and held it there for a couple of minutes. He pointed to another knotted muscle on the other side of his spine and I held the crystal against it as well. After five minutes, I asked him if he felt any different. He denied feeling any change. I apologized and wished him well.

The next day, he came to work with his back straight. When I asked him how he felt, he said, "Much better." He looked at me with a sheepish expression. "I have to admit I've never had such quick results before. I didn't even need to take painkillers last night."

My crystal has become a powerful healing tool. In addition to giving me greater healing power for my aches and pains, my special stone helps me remain serene and in a positive attitude. When family members are ill, I hold the crystal and think of their health changing to wellness. Then I relive the sensation that I experienced on top of Sedona's red rocks—a feeling of extraordinary well-being, and a knowledge that everything will happen as it should. The crystal is truly my sacred stone. ◯

Finding Forever

Rev. Karen Coussens

A QUAINT TOWN ON THE SHORES OF LAKE MICHIGAN, Petoskey is famous for its Petoskey Stone, a beautiful fossilized stone found only in that area of the lakeshore.

My prize souvenir from a childhood trip was a pendant made from a polished Petoskey stone in the shape of the mitten of Michigan. The necklace became my favorite accessory, not because of its shape but because the beauty of the Petoskey stone spoke gently to me of times past and a certain sense of the eternal.

Many years later, vacations with my own children took me back to Petoskey. We spent wonderful hours walking the beaches and shoreline searching for our own Petoskey stones. The searches were often fruitless, but they created many happy and fun-filled family memories, another touch of the stone's gift of "forever."

Recently, after a time of chaos in my life, I moved to the upper northwestern part of Michigan's lower peninsula. Now only sixty miles from Petoskey, I thought visits there would become frequent and finding the Petoskey stone of my own less elusive. But I didn't have time, focused as I was instead on setting up a new household, finding a job, creating a home, and establishing a life.

A year after moving in, my focus was on gardening, working with this land I was now caretaker for and that I loved deeply. Early one spring morning I walked outside, following the now familiar route of bird and animal feeding stations that I had established. Busily setting out feed, I plodded slowly, with my head bent, looking for interesting stones to place in the gardens I would soon be planting.

Just at the feeder in the large pine, I saw it. It had been a damp morning, and the dew still kept its surface wet, showing the fossil marks clearly. A Petoskey stone. It shouldn't have been here, not in this area—but it was.

With eyes much more damp than the morning, I bent to gently pick it up. Approximately the size of a hen's egg, it was perfect, marked on all sides. In awe I looked about, as if I could see who had placed it there for me. In that looking about, I saw the property I loved: the valley, the stream, the trees, the earth, the clear blue sky. I knew immediately Who had placed the stone at my feet. I whispered my thanks.

"My" Petoskey stone now rests in a little fountain in my bedroom where the water keeps its markings obvious. Also obvious is the lesson I learned—finding "forever" may not come as planned or dreamed; sometimes it is waiting at your feet to be found in one small step of joy. ◎

Rolling Stone

Warren Lane Molton

IT WAS BARELY DAYLIGHT WHEN THE MAJOR AND I drove around the boulder at the entrance to the motor pool, on our way to visit outlying units under his command and my care. "Hey, Chaplain, looks like a good'n," the major said, nodding at the sunrise.

Suddenly he braked his jeep and yelled to the Korean civilians waiting for their daily assignment. "When I come back tonight at chow time I want that damned rock outta here, understand? Gone! Got it?"

He sliced the air above his steering wheel and pointed at the boulder we had just passed. His heavy Southern accent did nothing to soften his order. We were both new to Korea and did not yet know the GI lingo that tortured the language to make us understood. But they seemed to understand anyway, and variously saluted and bowed to cover all their bases. The Koreans always seemed to have our number in any situation.

As we drove toward the gate of the compound, the major broke into laughter. "No way in hell they can move that thing. There's no equipment left to move anything with but a few jeeps." He chuckled.

"Wonder who the shave-tail was that stuck the motor pool there anyway. Idiot. Guess he thought it made a good island for directing traffic or something. Dumb!" he continued, choosing language he thought acceptable to his chaplain's ears.

We pulled into a cloud of dust from the heavy convoy that had just passed heading north. "Now, let's see. Where's that map?" he asked. I pulled it from under his seat, and he looked at me as if to say, "Glad you chaplains are good for something."

We returned at dusk, chatting about our trip. Suddenly, at the entrance to the motor pool, the major slammed on brakes.

"Holy Mary, Mother of God," this good Catholic exclaimed with his favorite oath in the presence of awe. "It's gone. Look, Chappy, the goddamn thing's really gone! Sorry, Chappy," he said, now trying to be a good boy.

We stared at the empty spot before us. The boulder had disappeared. The major looked back and forth from me to the road as though wanting an answer. Then he bounded out of the jeep for the motor pool tent yelling, "Sergeant, Sergeant Davis!"

As I was getting out, the corporal I had seen around the motor pool appeared from the direction of the mess hall. We greeted each other, and I asked, "You don't know what happened to the rock, do you?"

He laughed. "Funny thing, Chaplain. They just dug a big hole next to it, caved it in, covered it up, and hauled the dirt away in a wheelbarrow. Just like that. Nothing to it. Like they did it every day. Got a little scary there at the end, I thought. They took turns in the pit, chatting it up for courage I guess, like a Little League team. Could have buried one of them under that thing. They really were scrambling when the rock started sliding. Some trick. These guys are a lot smarter than we give 'em credit for," he said.

Ever the chaplain, I agreed and added, "Sometimes that's all we can do with something—bury it and remember it."

"Or forget it," he added.

He was moving to park the jeep when the major roared out of the tent shouting, "Hey, Chappy, wait up. I gotta miracle for you." ☺

One Rock

Anne Ewing Rassios

MY HUSBAND BROUGHT ME A FUNNY ROCK LAST fall.

He was plowing up the cornfields of a friend along the Venetikos River here in Greece, and this funny rock turned up. He wanted me to look at it.

As the only geoscientist in the area, people bring me funny rocks all the time. Funny-looking rocks, rocks with funny-looking fossils, rocks that, they claim, must have gold in them (!).

I take them all, people and rocks, quite seriously, and whip out my pocket microscope to examine these special stones. Most of the time, I really don't need the pocket microscope, but it looks impressive to the person who brought me the rock.

Nearly all the funny rocks brought to me are types local to my area, so I've seen them over and over again, and I know them nearly as well as I do my husband—perhaps even better. We've only been married twenty-five years, while the rocks and I have been together a lot longer.

I do my best to look at what some curious villager brings to me, grunt intelligently, and usually say some-thing like—*Well, this is really interesting! This is feldspar, and this pyroxene, but that one that shines like a metal in the light—yeah, isn't it pretty? But sorry, absolutely no gold in this rock. No, not worth a drachma. But it's really a very special rock. Once (upon a time), more than 175 million years ago—yeah really, it's that old!—this was a rock that came from beneath an ocean that doesn't exist anymore. A very special rock. . . .*

Sometimes, after a few months have gone by, I visit the friend who brought me the rock-without-gold-in-it, and I find he's put it in a special place on his mantelpiece.

It doesn't take gold to make a rock special.

That's what I say to a person who brings me a funny rock. What I say to myself in my field notes about similar rocks, about the funny and mundane rocks I look at up in the mountains, is not really that much more complex. Sometimes the person who brought me the rock is not so interested in it any more (since it contains no gold), and he leaves his pretty rock with me. I may pick up the pocket microscope again and take another peek, remembering the way a particular crystal glinted and flirted under my initial perusal.

The view into a rock with a pocket microscope is seductive. It's easy to be lead astray, seduced among the minerals, captivated by a view no human eye has ever seen before. It's altogether too easy to lose oneself among the facets, the miniature mountains, the colors that the earth itself is made of. I've often wondered why God hides this precious vision away from the view of most people. Perhaps we scientists are lucky.

The first time I ever looked inside a rock was when I bashed a pebble open using my dad's carpentry hammer. I must have been about seven. I don't know what possessed me to break it open. But I remember my first view inside. The mud-stained mundane surface gave way to an interior of fresh indigo, both dark and bright at the same time, a beautiful color I'd never seen before.

I took it to show my father, pleased with my pretty rock. Dad, who was a petroleum geologist, told me a story about the volcano this rock had once flowed out of. I was skeptical.

Since that day with Dad, I've seen and held rocks from the moon. I've cut and polished bits of meteors, examined their striations, sometimes odd and interesting, and imagined their formation in some planet or planetoid long ago in a galaxy far away.

Rocks are mountains made small. This is a simple and elegant concept. Usually the scale of my work encompasses entire mountains, and to study them I look at the rocks they're made from. To look at a rock is to see a mountain, or perhaps a mountain that once was, in miniature. Lots of rocks are made of older rocks that have been made into mountains more than once.

There are real metamorphic-magician geologists, some who earn an entire Ph.D. by analyzing a bit of rock smaller that a square inch. These scientists can trace a rock's origin farther than the latest mountain it finds itself within, into some long-forgotten mountains that were once, perhaps, higher than the Himalayas and that were once, perhaps, right here under your feet.

This, you must agree, is a special vision indeed. There is, as yet, no geological specialty that teaches you to look at a rock and envision the future mountains to which the rock might someday join its constituent parts—along with the parts that make you and me, our homes and lives. Eventually, we will all metamorphose into materials that can make mountains.

Let me tell you a bit about that rock my husband brought me.

One Rock

There's a favorite game geologists like to play. It works something like this: given a rock at random, describe the planet of its origin. It's not a bad way to approach the description of any old rock, be it a sample from the moon or Mars or from the cornfield by the river.

So, pocket microscope out, scanning the surface and broken open interior, here's my description of that rock, one rock:

• From the family of minerals, from their size, from their random attitude one toward another, I know this rock originated in the deep plumbing of a volcanic system. The planet of origin of this rock had volcanoes.

• The kind of volcanic system that makes these sorts of rocks comprises long arcs of volcanoes that are aligned within an ocean crust. Thus, the planet of origin has long-forgotten oceans; perhaps this rock could be the only remaining fragment of a once-grand ocean.

• Since the rock is no longer within a volcano, nor the volcano within the sea, this implies that some powerful tectonic force thrust the rock from its crib to a position within a mountain, up here, onto the face of the earth, into the sunlight, exposed to the view of all.

• But there is no mountain here alongside the river. Dislodged from the mountain, the rock made its way to us, riverborn, rolling, tumbling, carried by the floods of long-ago mountain streams. I can feel where part of the stone has been smoothed by the action of water and friction in a world that thus has air, rivers, and a climate favorable to life, to me, to people who like to look at rocks.

But this rock, even more special, even though broken, retains most of a cylindrical hole, bored through it in a manner of perfection that leaves me in awe. I carefully examine the hole and the rationally flattened body of the stone, trailing to a sharpened blade. I examine the artificial surface; I peer into the perfectly drilled hole with the pocket microscope.

I see polishing marks on this stone made by the hand of a Neolithic man, who worked this rock into a hand ax. I can imagine him by the river, poised over the gravel bed, searching the cobbles for just such a stone as this. I can imagine him squinting to examine the rock closely for imperfections that might cause it to break, to crack, to threaten the success of a hunt for game needed to sustain his family. Maybe he looked at the stone and was caught up in the colors of the earth itself. He, some 8,000 years ago, and I are the only ones to have carefully examined this rock, this special rock.

That's what you can learn from one rock. If you take the trouble to look. ◎

The Pebble Ring

Judy Ray

for David

Seven years ago
you gave me a white pebble
from the ocean,
a ring that spoke
of the sea's swelling
and of our love.
I lost the ring in the cold
white of icy Alps.
Perhaps it was carried back
with melting glaciers
to a beach of stones
where it goes on whispering
of love and of giving,
where new lovers will kneel.

The Buffalo Stone

Tonya Whitedeer Cargill

IT SEEMS LIKE AT LEAST A HUNDRED YEARS AGO, or perhaps another lifetime. I had been on a quest for answers with years of questions piled up in my mind. I read everything I could on ways of the ancient ones, trying to find something that would bring peace to my heart. I was filled with yearning for that silent comfort that many other people seem to have. Those who don't have this comfort know what it is to have a huge emptiness deep within the soul.

It was a beautiful spring day. Lavender, feverfew, lobelia, and the huge yellow rosebush were in full bloom. The pond's gentle water hyacinths had multiplied, and their spikes of purple flowers floated slowly with a slight breeze. Butterflies fluttered everywhere, and I was lost in thought, pondering why was I here.

What was this wondrous energy that keeps the whole universe in a harmonious flow? As my thoughts flew from my yearning place, I noticed butterflies flying in a circle around my head. I kicked the water with my toe and a rainbow flew out of the water and arched over the side of the pond. I took a closer look. The end of the rainbow seemed to be connected to a stone in the bottom of the pond—a stone emitting a brilliant light.

I tried to reach into the water, but it was too deep. Not wanting to disturb the koi, I ran into the house and got my salad tongs. I reached in and grabbed that mystical white stone.

I almost dropped it. It was a pure white buffalo with a face that smiled at me. This was not a precise shape, not a form anyone had deliberately carved, but it was definitely a white buffalo. "This is a sign," my inner voice said.

I studied all the information I could find on the white buffalo, and the Native American legend of the White Buffalo Woman. To my surprise it became a door opening the way to spiritual connection. It gave me my totem name. From that day forward, I knew I had found my native heritage.

Do I believe now? There is no doubt in my mind that we are all connected, and that when I need a question answered—when I seek truth—it will be revealed. It is our responsibility to know the signs, the clues, the hidden things that the Creator plants for us to find. ✑

Perfect Fit

Denise E. Richards

It was sweet September, the day before my birthday. With my lover of a year, I traveled to Morro Bay, midway along California's sprawling coastline. The house we had borrowed for the weekend sat on a tiny dead-end street paralleling the coast. A rolling sand plateau separated it from the shore a hundred yards away. Fat succulents fanned out like invading armies, surrounding each sage-crowned hillock and overrunning the narrow path that wandered through the lumpy landscape.

Near the beach, the path vanished in a patch of rocks and crumbled sandstone. Just beyond, a crest of dunes rose abruptly in soft, sandy splendor, braced against the storms and the high tides. It had taken two laden trips to haul everything we imagined wanting for our magical day together. At last, the drudgery was done and the ecstasy could begin.

We roved the shallow sand eddies and chose a private spot for our love nest. Spreading out a soft plaid blanket, we weighed down the corners with our luggage—a daypack, a book of poems, a bamboo tray, boom box, and cooler. All the essentials were at the ready—grapes, ice water, sharp cheese, and champagne. We sat close and inhaled the living blessing of sea air. A flock of snowy gulls stood hunched before the gusting breeze, shifting now and then to replace one another, like chess pieces or the queen's watch.

We are devotees of beauty, Charles and I, champions of truth, imbuers of meaning, patrons of ritual, celebrators of the sublime. This was a day dedicated to our love and to all these things.

We luxuriated in our cozy open fort, soaking up the crisp light, the clear sharp sounds of the birds, and the rumble of the surf. After awhile, we fledged from our intimate nest. Our brief excursions always ended back at our blanket, and we danced around it, finding each other, embracing and resting in the sentient sanctuary of the other's eyes. We laughed and drank chilled sunshine from our flutes. We kissed, losing ourselves in the divine gift of each other.

In the afternoon we ventured further down the beach, strolling blissfully along the shore. Hand in hand, each step filled us with a sense of well being. In this state of grace, everything around us was dazzling, yet serene. Finally, we made our way back. Treasure-hunting along the flotsam line where the water strained to make landfall, we delighted in our finds.

One such prize was a simple stone. It was dove gray, smooth and heavy, with a grainy texture, like a miniature boulder the size of my palm but bearing one jagged face—a russet potato, petrified, then chiseled in two. The outside surfaces were worn and rounded and lightened from exposure. The rough interior face was a stormy gray, faceted with hard edges and small planes, little overhangs and shallow indentations. We were struck by the contrasts in its color and lines, and Charles picked it up.

When we reached our beach nest, we rested for a while, enjoying the enchantment of our chosen spot before heading back to the house where we could enjoy absolute privacy. With an armful of belongings, we forged a virgin pass through the dunes, feeling high and light and wonderful.

Traveling lazily beyond the dunes, something made me glance down, and in an instant synapses sizzled, consciousness and recognition gathered in a leap. I let out a little gasp as I pointed to the rock at my feet.

I flashed Charles a look of astonishment as I bent to pick it up. Understanding, he smiled and said gently, "No, honey, it couldn't be," not wanting me to be disappointed. But I knew. I don't know how, but I knew, immediately, and with certainty. My hair and spine tingled in rapture. Charles gamely pulled the other rock from his pocket, and confidently, reverently, I raised my piece to his. Yes. It was. Each protrusion nested snugly in the other's hollow, each depression and facet was exquisitely met by a matching contusion—every nook, every cranny, was mirrored in chalky form, and the halves came together like carved bookends. The fit was complete, there was absolutely nothing missing. It was perfect.

The two halves of this simple stone had lain a half mile apart, in completely different terrains—one far down the beach in the damp sand near the waterline, the other up over the dune barrier, off the trail and lost amid myriad broken rocks and scattered vegetation. We stared at each other in speechless wonder.

That evening, we held a ceremony on the deck under the stars. We bathed our special stone in a glazed bowl of cerulean blue. The broken stone was such a poignant metaphor for the miracle of love—two people coming together, unexpectedly, from contrasting walks of life, experience, and homelands, from complex circles and disparate circumstances, at a random crossing. Sometimes a soul mate appears in a place you wouldn't have thought to look, or more importantly, in a form you wouldn't recognize.

I know that under ordinary circumstances, we would never have discovered that second stone—if our hearts and souls were not completely open to the heavens and to one another. That moonlit night, we left the stone halves resting together in cool water, facing one another, but just apart.

Six months later, Charles and I married on a bluff high above the crashing surf along Mendocino's rugged shoreline. The two halves of the stone played as great a role in our ceremony as the rings we exchanged. We slowly approached one another, each bearing one part of the stone, and stood drinking deeply of the tenderness in each other's eyes. We united the halves of our sacred stone, and held them, rejoined, as we said our vows.

Charles and I do not believe we became "one" that day, but, rather, that we celebrated the precious and essential wholeness we *each* experience, basking in the deep love of the other. We pledged to make our lives' journey together, to make it artful and intentional, to fill our days with discovery as we explore our potentials and the wonders of the world, creating a life rich in beauty and meaning.

Our sacred stones rest near one another in a place of honor, on a simple jade tray. We include them in anniversary celebrations and other treasured times when we feel the call to renew the deep connection they represent for us. They will always be an inimitable reminder of our extraordinary good fortune in having found one another. ☺

Duality
Colleen Palmer

Solid like a stone
Your strength gives rise to my tune
   as I pour myself
    over
     you
Water in a brook

A Message from Beyond
Martha H. Gill

FOR AS LONG AS I CAN REMEMBER, MOM LOVED nature. She fed the birds in the winter and tended her flower gardens in the summer. She grew up in the Northeast and had a special affinity for the rocky New England coast, where she collected stones, shells, and shards of weathered beach glass.

She continued her passion when she moved to southwest Florida. Mom bought every book available about subtropical flora and fauna and often spent weekends exploring the Everglades, Corkscrew Swamp, and other regional wildlife refuges. She loved walking along the Gulf Coast beaches as much as those of her beloved New England.

When Mom learned that she had terminal cancer, too advanced for treatment, her mood was calm. She had lived a happy, healthy, full life and wasn't afraid of death, even though she didn't have a religious belief in the soul or an afterlife.

When she started to fail, we knew it was a matter of days. Jennifer, who lived in Seattle, had a special connection with her grandmother because of their mutual love, interest in, and respect for all living things. The night Mom died, Jennifer was flying in to see her for one last time. She missed her by just one hour.

Jennifer was very upset that she hadn't had a chance to say a final goodbye to her grandmother. But the next day, as she walked along the beach at the water's edge—

the very beach her grandmother had walked hundreds of times—she felt something hard hit her ankle, despite the fact that it was such a calm day the waves had been gently lapping at her feet.

She looked down. There in the water at her feet was a perfect heart-shaped stone! She knew her grandmother had sent it to her. Mom had found her spiritual connection to the universe and had chosen the perfect way to say goodbye—and hello—to her granddaughter. ☙

Joining the Circle
Gordon Haynes

FAINT BIRD SONGS HAVE WAKENED ME AT 5:00 A.M. My alarm is set for six, but I move mechanically to dress anyway, strange for me. I venture carefully out into the predawn darkness of Shantivanam's Forest of Peace Retreat Center. I have come to soak up the silence and sounds of nature, to find spiritual solace, and to find a center that holds and confirms the *imago dei* (the godly image) within.

The great gray stones of the circle of monoliths I sat within last evening speak my name. *Sunrise is coming, join us.* I begin the half-mile walk to the hilltop, winding along a path through a waist-high sea of hay grasses. The evening rain has called the morning dew, giving the whole world a green carpet of moisture that rises up through my shoes.

Finally, I enter the circle, twelve giant stones unearthed in the digging of the retreat center's foundation and magically, it seems, transported to this clearing. They stand precariously on end, held upright by some equally magical spell. I sit in the center on a simple wooden bench, cool dampness against my jeans. Hay ready for mowing flows out in all directions, surrounded by trees in the distance. Resting in this strong center, I feel the power of this private place. I wait. The sun begins to glow above the tree line. Streaks of magentas and royal blues spill onto the moist grasses.

My verbal prayer from the evening before, Psalm 139, which I had offered to these stones with abandon and the rhetoric of a full heart, still hangs over this sacred place. My shouts of joy at the wonder that *You, O God, knew me and shaped me in my mother's womb*, still reverberate among the circled stones.

Then, from some instinct, I rise and move to the right to get a better look at the brightening sun. I realize I am standing in the circle's circumference, filling an empty place. In that moment I become a stone, witnessing, like my brothers and sisters, the breathless moment of light breaking the darkness.

For the next half hour I am a stone, standing still, feeling my great substance, anchored in the ground. I am a stone, joining the silent sentinels of this circle. I feel a deep connection with the earth, the sun, and all of creation. I have not asked for this gift. It surprises me with its firm insistence that I am a welcomed part of this place, of life itself, even the primordial existence of my stone companions.

A bobwhite acknowledges the dawn. Our circle gazes in awe at the familiar mystery of light illuminating darkness. With peace and reverence, I accept this unexpected gift of union with the earth's ancient cycle.

As I walk down the path, I look back to that space I filled for a few short moments. Yes, the center holds. It holds. The *imago dei* within me has bestowed the briefest glimpse of the face of God. ☺

Rocks at Rising Sun
Maya

Oh the waters
rushing make us
come alive, sing our mineral names
oga, weah, steh,
our grey black faces we offer
along the banks
for your next step

Half face, quarterface,
smoothed by centuries of river
and ice mother before her,
who inscribed her name
in our veins

We are old as Earth, born of dream-story
and mist, in love with rushing
thighs, having lost the patience of glaciers
as water's children
have forgotten the song
stillness is

Stone Elders

Bob Liebert

BACK IN THE SIXTEENTH CENTURY, A JESUIT ASKED a medicine man if he really thought that the stones were alive and had a spirit. The medicine man thought a long time and finally answered: "Some are." Obvious proof of their naive simplicity, said the Jesuit, to whom the stones were dead in all senses forever.

In Native American lore, stones are directly materialized from the fires and stars of the universe, which of course they are, a part of the original Creation. They are the Eldest. They have seen many ages of the Earth and will endure even when we are gone. They are the foundation of Grandmother Earth. They are the strength of our bones; indeed, we are literally of them, of stardust.

Some stone spirits can work with us in teaching us, and we will be led to these stones. To work with one or two is plenty. Let them find you. Take years until you are sure, if need be. Never carelessly remove a stone from its home. Stones can give us good thoughts and also appear in our dreams. Stones are known to suddenly appear in a ceremony. Stones are known to teleport as well as to move over the ground.

My own sacred stone came to me before a Sun Dance in North Dakota. It is one of the few traditional ceremonies in that area in which Native Americans allow white people inside the Circle. During the evening, after eating the last little feast, we dancers spent some time digesting our food and reflecting on the long road to our next meal. It was also a good time to remember why we were dancing that sacrifice.

In the dying light, I set off to walk along one side of the high butte. I hadn't gone too far before a rattlesnake convinced me to wander in another direction, and I headed to the opposite side of the butte.

The commotion of the Sun Dance was above me. Just ahead of my feet I noticed a reddish, semitranslucent rock. It spoke to me. I decided, though, to be very sure. We can take nothing into the Sun Dance, so I left it there, and thought to myself, "If this is all real, I will be able to find the stone again."

After many experiences in the dance, we took our first shower in two weeks down in the highway town on the reservation. I tested my resolve by making the two friends who had driven with me to the Dakotas take me all the way back up on the butte.

I had trouble even remembering where I sat that day but wound up walking right to the stone. Even so, I noticed a distinct little track that marked where the stone had moved, a distance of about three feet. There had been no rain. I put down tobacco and made an earnest prayer before removing the stone.

I try to care for my stone; I don't always feel worthy of the gift. Stones are powerful. They can be used to release things we wish to get rid of, and they can be held or applied for strength and healing. Things that are supposedly simple, like stones, can lead us back to our lost spiritual senses and back to the Sacred Earth that is our true home.

When I go out on a fast, I take my stone with me. It has many pictures on it, and they frequently change, becoming more or less distinct. There is a Sun Dance Tree and lightning. A fox appears. Spirit faces appear.

Not long ago, the goofiest-looking guy appeared on my stone and I had to laugh: a sacred clown for balance. He reminded me that with heart and humor and humility, we can be at peace with our imperfections. ◯

In Defense of My Stone
Judith A. Stock

Reasoning people tell me
a stone does not
communicate
in any manner,
nor does it feel
or understand.

I have decided
to take my stone
somewhere
where it can.

When a Stone Chooses You

Charo Tataje de Baixarias

I FELT THAT THE POSSESSION OF A QUARTZ STONE would help me in my spiritual journey, but how could I obtain one without buying it? I wanted to receive it as a gift from other hands.

I told my friend, Andres, about the benefits and power of quartz, and we decided to look for a quartz stone together. As we walked through the city toward the market area, we saw an older woman on a busy street corner—an unusual place to sell wares. She wore the traditional dress of native Indians from the mountainous area of Cuzco.

We watched as she unfolded a red blanket-sized *manta* on the sidewalk and spread out many different quartz stones. One caught my attention. I felt like it was calling me. In fact, I felt an irresistible attraction. It was large, twelve inches long and six inches high, and pure white, with flecks of gold near the base.

"How much?" I asked.

She looked at me with a gentle twinkle in her eyes. Her ruddy cheeks and clear complexion made her seem ageless.

"Ten soles," she said.

The price was lower than we expected to pay for a stone of this size and quality. She told us that the quartz came from the mountain of Machu Picchu.

I knew this stone needed to find its home with me. Andres and I decided to pay half each, cut the stone in two, and exchange halves. In this way, the stone would be a gift rather than a purchase.

The woman wanted to cut it in half to satisfy our wish, and tried several times, but she couldn't. Silently, without saying so, I sent my spirit inside the rock, asking permission to divide it.

"Try it one more time," I urged. The woman cut it easily right down the middle. *This is the natural way,* the stone seemed to say, *to ask permission to do what we need to do in life.*

She handed the two halves of the stone to us. Andres offered his half to me and I did the same for him. I explained how to cleanse it, first with sea water, then by exposing it to moonlight for three consecutive nights.

We Peruvians know the Incan wisdom about the use of quartz. This beautiful stone takes centuries to condense its light into matter and to pass from color to color, because in nature every color has its own force and effect. In this way, the quartz stones help us to progress with our body or our spirit, depending on what our needs are.

"After the cleansing, you can program the stone," I told Andres. "Let the stone know what its purpose is in your life, what you want it to help you with."

My family and friends marveled at the powers of my quartz. They wanted to find one from the same area. But though they went to the same corner of the city, they never found the *vieja* who sold it to us.

Several years passed, and I had many beautiful spiritual experiences with my half of the stone. But the two halves were destined, it seems, to be reunited. After six years, my friend Andres became my husband. The two pieces are together again. When a stone chooses you, she stays with you, forever. ◎

Meditation
How to Let a Stone Choose You

There are many ways to let a stone come into your life. Here are some general suggestions for how to perceive which stones might benefit you. Approach the task from a place of openness and love. Declare your intention to "meet" the right stone for you, and be ready to receive it.

If you find a reputable store that displays and sells gemstones, ask the owner for recommendations. This person may have vast knowledge of stones and their uses. Many shopkeepers will tell you about their own experiences with certain stones.

As you roam the shop, notice which stones you seem drawn to. If you use a pendulum or other guidance, use it with individual stones or, if drawn to several, with stones in groups of three or four at a time (more might be confusing).

Consider the purpose for your stone. Certain stones are known for their healing properties; others may work with relationships, create abundance, or increase mental clarity. Some stones, such as quartz crystal, enhance and amplify whatever energy is directed through them.

Here is a checklist of other things to consider:

• Is the surface of the stone smooth or rough? Depending on the purpose, you may want one kind or the other. If the stone is smooth, has it been mechanically tumbled? (Some people believe that this weakens the natural life force of the stone.) Or is it smoothed from the natural action of waves or sand?

• What size and shape is the stone? Bigger is not necessarily better. You may want a stone that feels good to hold or one with a flat side to lay on the body. Heart-shaped stones or "holey" stones (those with holes naturally made) have their own significance.

• What is the origin of the stone? Different mineral contents and molecular densities create varied energy fields.

• What color is the stone? Colors can be coordinated with chakras (the body's energy centers) or with other symbology. Green stones, for instance, may be used to enhance prosperity, abundance, and growth. Blue or purple stones may magnify spiritual direction and purpose. See the meditation, "Stone Colors and What They Mean," in Part II (page 116). Excellent resources exist through books on gemstones.

• How well does the stone hold heat? This may be an important factor if you want to use heated stones in massage or other bodywork.

Before you go to a store or walk on a beach to look at stones, you may find it helpful to do the meditation on the next page.

A Stone Journey

In a quiet place, with pen and paper near, close your eyes, relax your body, and sit quietly. Let your thoughts go. Set your intention to go on a meditative stone journey. Take yourself to a deep, wooded forest. As you wander through the forest, you see the mouth of a cave, and you enter a deep underground cavern, with many beautiful stones lying in all directions. Notice the colors, shapes, sizes, and vibrations of the stones. Listen for any stones that may call to you.

Begin walking toward the stones. As you walk, notice your emotional response. Does this stone want to be with you? Do you want to be with it? Take your time, and walk among the stones as long as you like.

Finally, allow at least one stone to choose you. Open your eyes. Write whatever this stone tells you about why it has chosen you, what it can help you with, and why it wants to be in your life.

Contributors

Paul W. Anderson, Ph.D., a licensed psychologist in private practice, helps people connect with their own inner powers. "Learning how to trust ourselves and follow the light that shines from the inside out is the biggest challenge in life." Contact him through his Web site at *www.netpsychologist.com*. ℂ

Robert M. "Bob" Anderson, Ph.D., is currently a chief master sergeant in the U.S. Air Force Reserve, assigned to the 917th Bomb Wing at Barksdale Air Force Base, Louisiana. He holds Ph.D.s in human resource management and safety management, a master's degree in police science, and a bachelor's degree in social psychology. He is a motivational speaker on leadership, communication, motivation, service, and relationships, and is founder and president of Back to Basics International. Contact him at *www.yackityak.com*. ℂ

George Arbeitman is a native of Brooklyn, New York. His parents were first-generation European immigrants. He draws inspiration for his writing from his family, his ethnic neighborhood, and his dreams. He is a contributor to several volumes of the Riverside Poetry workshop chapbooks. Contact him at *Karlgalra@hotmail.com*. ℂ

Michelle Auerbach is a writer living in Boulder, Colorado. She has published her work variously in journals, on the Internet, has written stories, poetry, novels, pieces of long projective prose, and done translations from various languages, mostly dead ones. If she had the same magic powers she possessed as a child, she would levitate Boulder and move it back to New York. Contact her at *michelle.auerbach@pobox.com*. ℂ

Charo Tataje de Baixarias is a native of Peru, born the fifth of seven children. She has had "amazing and beautiful experiences" of spiritual connection and healing since childhood and says, "God, love, and the Universe are my guides." Contact her at *charobaixarias@ yahoo.com.* ◯

Walter Bargen has published ten books of poetry. His two most recent are *The Body of Water* (Timberline Press) and *The Feast* (BkMk Press-UMKC), both published in 2003. His poems have appeared in *The Iowa Review, Boulevard, Beloit Poetry Journal, Notre Dame Review,* and *New Letters.* He was the winner of the Chester H. Jones Foundation prize in 1997. He can be contacted at *www. walterbargen.com.* ◯

Phyllis Becker is a graduate of Howard University and works in human services. She is on the board of The Writer's Place, Inc., and is involved in literary outreach to area schools. Her poems have been published in *Kansas Quarterly, Cottonwood, Uncle, TIWA, Thorny Locust, Any Key Review, Kansas City Star,* and *Fathers: A Collection of Poems* (St. Martin's Press). Her chapbook is *Walking Naked into Sunday* (Wheel of Fire Press). Contact her at *pebpoet@hotmail.com.* ◯

Kathleen Craft Boehmig, a native Atlantan, loves writing about her Southern heritage. She lives with her husband and seven-year-old son in Roswell, Georgia. She writes feature pieces for local periodicals and is working on a book of essays. Her nonfiction essay about September 11, 2001, won placement in *O Georgia!,* an annual anthology. Contact her at *pkboehmig@charter.net.* ◯

Joyce Brady is a holistic health educator, writer, and photographer. She facilitates "wise women's circles" using poetry and symbolism as vehicles for awareness. She consults symbols for organizations and individuals and teaches ongoing "Symbolic Awareness" workshops. Her poems and essays have been published in journals and anthologies. She loves to travel. Contact her at *sacredintention@cs.com.*

Regina Murray Brault lived for thirteen years in Barre, Vermont, which locals call "Granite Capital of the World." Her poetry has appeared in several publications, including *The Comstock Review, Poet,* and *Midwest Poetry Review.* She has received numerous state and national awards, including the 1996 Clark College Award for Poetry and the 1997 San Francisco Dancing Poetry Competition Grand Prize. Contact her at *regina150@hotmail.com.*

Ted T. Cable Ph.D., Professor of Park Management and Conservation at Kansas State University, has worked on nature conservation projects in more than twenty U.S. states as well as Canada, Latin America, and Africa. He is author of *Commitments of the Heart: Odysseys in West African Conservation,* four other books, and more than 150 articles. His book, *Interpretation for the 21st Century: Fifteen Guiding Principles for Interpreting Nature and Culture,* has also been published in Chinese. Contact him at *tcable@oznet.ksu.edu.*

Tonya Whitedeer Cargill lives in the mountains of Northern California in a town of 1,500. She and her husband, Threecrows, are dedicated to growing herbs, especially endangered medicinal plants. Their ten acres, Medicine Creek, provide them "the peace and serenity that we require for not only growing herbs but also for our business of handcrafting Native American–style beaded leather products." She writes and teaches for the healing of Mother Earth. Contact her at *whitebuffalowoman@ msn.com.* ◎

Ava Chambers grew up in the mountains of Northeast Georgia. Blessed with cold streams, rich fields, and glorious hills, she learned appreciation for the earth and its treasures. Writing brings great satisfaction. Her work can be found in several inspirational publications. She is an active member in the National League of American Pen Women, Georgia Writers, Inc., and the Atlanta Writers Club. She lives in Acworth, Georgia with her husband and four children. Contact her at *acham922@aol.com.* ◎

Dru Clarke grew up in New Jersey and spent summers between the highlands and the shore, learning to love those landscapes in between. Originally in social work, she later became a science teacher, concentrating on marine science and ecology. She lives in the Flint Hills of northeast Kansas with her husband, a herd of over twenty quarter horses, three dogs, many cats, and some chickens. Contact her at *druc@kansas.net.* ◎

Patricia Clothier grew up on a ranch in the wilds of West Texas, taught art and language arts, and with her husband, Grant, built and operated a children's camp in the Missouri Ozarks for twenty years. These experiences enhanced her love for nature and young people. Patricia is author of *Beneath the Window* (Iron Mountain Press, 2003), a narrative of ranch life in Big Bend country before that area became a national park. Contact her at *PnGClothier@aol.com*. ✑

SuzAnne C. Cole, former college English instructor, wrote *To Our Heart's Content: Meditations for Women Turning Fifty*. She's also published more than 200 works of poetry, fiction, and essays in a wide range of anthologies and commercial and literary publications, including *Newsweek*, the *Houston Chronicle*, the *Baltimore Sun*, and *Writer's Digest*. Her plays have been produced in New York City and Houston. She collects stones on all of her travels. Contact her at *SuzAnneCC@aol.com*. ✑

Rev. Karen Coussens's delight is her gift for storytelling, discovered as the mother of six, enhanced as the grandmother of nineteen, and great-grandmother of one. Now living in a yurt on eighty acres in northwest Michigan, Karen is learning new stories daily—stories of joy and peace in connecting with nature. She may be contacted at *kaycee@coslink.net*. ✑

Barbara Crooker has published over 1,000 poems in magazines such as *Yankee*, the *Christian Science Monitor*, *Smartish Pace*, and the *Denver Quarterly*; anthologies, including *Worlds in Their Words: An Anthology of Contemporary American Women Writers* (Prentice Hall), and eleven chapbooks. She has received three Pennsylvania Council on the Arts Fellowships in Literature, sixteen Pushcart Prize nominations, and was awarded the Thomas Merton Poetry of the Sacred Award in 2003. Contact her through her Web site at *www.barbaracrooker.com*. ✑

Contributors

Joy Cummings lives in Moorpark, California, and Port Townsend, Washington. She is the mother of five sons. She believes messages are all around us if we only learn to listen. In 2002, she and her husband, Curran, rode a tandem bicycle across America. She is writing a book about their adventure titled *See a Penny, Pick It Up*, for found coins literally guided them on their journey. Contact her at *jocurr02@yahoo.com*. ☺

Janet Cunningham, Ph.D. is an internationally known board-certified specialist in regression therapy, transpersonal counselor, and author. She is owner of *Breakthroughs to the Unconscious*®, a private practice in Columbia, Maryland; president of *Heritage Authors™*; and past president of the International Association for Regression Research and Therapies, Inc. Contact her at *www.janetcunningham.com*. ☺

J. P. Dancing Bear's poems have been published in *Verse Daily, Atlanta Review, Seattle Review, Poetry International, Permafrost,* and others. He is editor-in-chief of *The DMQ Review* and host of *Out of Our Minds,* a weekly poetry program on public radio station KKUP. He is winner of the 2002 Slipstream Press Poetry Prize for his chapbook, *What Language*. His full-length collection, *Billy Last Crow,* was published in 2004 by Turning Point Press. Contact him at *bearlaughing@yahoo.com*. ☺

Tony D'Arpino currently lives in San Francisco. His books include *The Shape of The Stone* and *Seven Dials*. His poetry has appeared in the *Bloomsbury Review, Crossconnect, Branches, Chaminade Literary Review,* and *Runes,* among others. An excerpt from his novel, *St Bonaventure's Island,* appears in *Terra Incognita* (Madrid). He has been poet-in-residence at Centrum and the Djerassi Foundation. Contact him at *tonydarpino@netscape.net.* ◎

Will Davis is of Native American heritage and spends a lot of his time engaged in Native activities. He is an artist and writer. Will tries to walk a spiritual path and as part of that path likes to share some of his journey with others from time to time. It is his hope that this story will help others with a ray of hope or encouragement. ◎

Phylameana lila Désy is a writer, Web publisher, and Usui reiki master. She operates a home-based healing practice in Southeastern Iowa. She is author of *The Everything® Reiki Book* (Adams Media, 2004). She also runs the popular Holistic Healing Guide site at About. com (*http://healing.about.com*), which features articles, information, and an international support community interested in all aspects of healing the mind-body-soul. Visit her Web site at *www.spiralvisions.com.* ◎

Peggy Eastman is the author of *Godly Glimpses: Discoveries of the Love That Heals,* and editor of *Share* magazine, a spiritual quarterly. Her work has appeared in many publications, including *SELF; New Choices* (a *Reader's Digest* publication), *New Age, Guideposts, His Mysterious Ways* (a *Guideposts* anthology), *Family Circle, Washingtonian, The Circle Continues* (an anthology of women's writing), and many others. She has received an award for poetry from Writer's Digest. Read more about *Godly Glimpses* on the Web site *www.bookviews. com/BookPage/godlyglimpses.html.* ◎

John R. Ellis' active spiritual path began when he sustained back injuries in 1986. In addition to studying shamanism and Native American healing traditions, he is a practicing reiki master, also incorporating feather and stone healings, together with toning and color therapy. He conducts long distance Spirit releases for those in need. Contact him at *jvliad@msn.com*. ◎

Margo Fallis, born in Edinburgh, Scotland, with a lust for adventure, has spent most of her life traveling. When she's not exploring the world, she's writing about her experiences. Margo studies world history and ancient cultures, is teaching herself to read and write Chinese, and does watercolor and drawing. Married and mother of five children, Margo writes children's stories for her seven grandchildren. Her adventures keep her young at heart! Contact her at *margofallis@yahoo.com*. ◎

Maureen Tolman Flannery was raised on a Wyoming mountain sheep ranch, where she developed a close and long-term relationship with stones. Her first book was *Secret of the Rising Up: Poems of Mexico*, and she edited the anthology *Knowing Stones: Poems of Exotic Places*. Her poems have appeared in more than 100 journals and anthologies, including *Atlanta Review*, *Amherst Review*, *Comstock Review*, *The Pagan's Muse*, *Intimate Kisses*, and *Woven on the Wind*. ◎

Terry Forde lives in Nevada, writes poetry, and is working on her first novel. Since her years at Santa Clara University, California, she has collected a desk full of personal jottings on life and draws much of her poetry from these life experiences. She is a member of the Ash

Canyon Poets and has been published in anthologies, newspapers, calendars, and magazines. Contact her at *newchapter-3@juno.com*. ☺

Shirley Fritchoff is an art and sand-tray therapist. She has lived on the Sea of Cortez in San Carlos, Sonora, Mexico for twenty years. Here she discovered natural runes from the sea. She leads small groups in therapeutic journal writing in Mexico and Tucson, Arizona. Contact her at *shirleyfritchoff@earthlink.net*. ☺

Martha H. Gill is an interior decorator and certified Feng Shui consultant. She also consults on healthy home design for people who are concerned about our environment and for those who can't tolerate chemicals used in the building process. Contact her at *gillinteriors@earthlink. net*. ☺

Jennifer Goodenberger is a concert pianist, composer, and visual artist. Her inspirations are sacred sites, stones, archetypal symbols, and designs from ancient and world cultures. As a pianist, her original works range from deeply healing and spiritual compositions to passionate and romantic creations. To learn more about her two CDs of original piano solos (*Return* and *Mystical*), and to see her artwork, visit her Web site at *www.jennifergoodenberger.com*. ☺

Susan Elizabeth Hale, singer, poet, and music therapist, is author of the forthcoming book, *Sacred Space—Sacred Sound*, as well as *Song and Silence: Voicing the Soul* (La Alameda Press, 1995). Susan teaches workshops and classes throughout the United States, Great Britain, and Canada, and directs *The Voice of the Rose: Songkeeper Apprenticeship Program* in Taos, New Mexico. Contact her at *www.angelfire.com/nm/susong.*

Carolyn A. Hall enjoys her Kansas farm heritage and newfound hobby, stonescaping. She writes memoir, satire, and mystery, which is also a good description of her life. She shares a river bluff residence with husband John and a little boy in a puppy suit named Jessie.

Sande Hart is founder of SARAH (Spiritual and Religious Alliance for Hope), a group of multicultural women formed to combat post–September 11, 2001, fear and prejudice by allowing women to come together in dialogue and community service. This experience has taught her "how easy it is to make a difference in the world when you come from the heart." She also believes that "when you come from the heart, magic happens." Visit the group's Web site at *www.sarah4hope.org.*

Gordon Haynes is a writer of poems and a searcher of inner space. After a career in the corporate world, he studied counseling psychology and is currently completing studies in spiritual direction at the Sophia Center at Mount Saint Scholastica Monastery in Atchison, Kansas. He has begun a ministry using the ancient practice of spiritual direction and companionship, walking with others in their journeys of the spirit. Contact him at *www.spiritlifetransitions.com.*

Anne Heath was born in Bronxville, New York, and received degrees from Sarah Lawrence College and Antioch University. She is author of *Between Earth* and Sky: Poets of the Cowboy West (WW Norton & Co, Inc.), winner of Western Heritage Award. A writer, poet, and fine artist, she currently lives in Bridgewater, Connecticut. ⌀

Penelope Holder was born into a theatrical and creative family and has always been interested in the arts, drawing, painting, acting, and writing. She is a member of the Roswell (Georgia) Fine Arts Alliance as well as the Atlanta Writers' Club. She writes short stories and inspirational nonfiction. Contact her at *penhold@bellsouth.net.* ⌀

Mary-Lane Kamberg is author of seven nonfiction books, including *The I Don't Know How to Cook Book* (Adams Media, 2004), and hundreds of articles and poems. She served as president of Whispering Prairie Press and fiction editor for the literary magazine, *Potpourri.* She received the 1996 James P. Immroth Memorial Award from the American Library Association's Intellectual Freedom Roundtable. Her biography appears in *Who's Who in America.* ⌀

William Keener is a writer and environmental lawyer living in the San Francisco Bay Area. His poems have appeared in numerous literary reviews, and his chapbook *Three Crows Yelling,* coauthored with Bill Noble and Michael Day, won the 1999 National Looking Glass Award from Pudding House Publications. His men's group, meeting monthly for the past eighteen years, created a closing ritual that is the subject of his poem. Contact him at *bkeener52@aol.com.* ⌀

Contributors

Ted Kooser, Poet Laureate, lives near the village of Garland, Nebraska, and teaches poetry writing at the University of Nebraska. His poems have appeared in *The New Yorker, Hudson Review, Antioch Review, Kenyon Review,* and others. Among other honors are the Hugo Prize (*Poetry Northwest*), the Kunitz Prize (Columbia), and *Shenandoah's* Boatwright Prize, as well as two National Endowment fellowships. He has authored nine collections of poetry and nine chapbooks and special editions, including *Delights & Shadows* (Copper Canyon Press, 2004). ◔

Ruth M. Laughlin received her B.A. and M.F.A. degrees in sculpture at Portland State University and Arizona State University. She has taught special education in the White Mountains of Arizona and coordinated programs for The Center for Blindness and Low Vision. Ruth expresses concepts and experiences through poetry and sculpture. She enjoys outdoor activities and exploring Native American spirituality and the healing arts. ◔

Patricia Lay-Dorsey lives in Detroit, Michigan, and describes herself as an artist/activist/writer. She is also a political satire-singer with the Raging Grannies Without Borders, song circle-lover, online photojournal keeper, woman-oriented festi-goer, and jazz nut. And you can't leave out her gratitude for time spent with children of Muslim Arab heritage in an art classroom every week in East Dearborn. She finds that being differently abled just makes life more interesting! Contact her at *www.windchimewalker.com.* ◔

Alison Leonard has written fiction for children and plays for BBC radio in Great Britain. All her life she has written sporadic poems when they have "come"; but since she moved toward an earth-based, goddess-oriented spirituality, the poems have come more often and consistently. Her poetry has been published in the *Edinburgh Review* and in U.K. anthologies, as well as in *The Friendly Woman* in the United States. Contact her at *www.alisonleonard.co.uk.* ☙

Karen Lee Lewis is a contributing editor for *Traffic East Magazine* (*www.trafficeast.com*) and a teaching artist for Just Buffalo Literary Center in Buffalo, New York. She edited *The Shadow's Imprint: Poetic Reflections on Death* (Blarney Stone Books). She teaches workshops on developing writing groups and has an essay in *The Writing Group Book* (Chicago Review Press). Her poetry, prose, and photography have appeared throughout the US and Canada. Contact her at *Kleelew@aol.com.* ☙

Bob Liebert, inspired by Native American ways from a young age, was fortunate to have been taught by Mandan and Lakota elders and has participated in many ceremonies. He is a practicing herbalist and member of the American Herbalist Guild. He lives with his wife, Jan, and family in a wild corner of the Missouri Ozarks. He is author of *Two Ravens, Osage Life and Legends,* and *Medicinal Herbs of the Ozarks.* Contact him at *www. teetercreekherbs.com.* ☙

Denise Low teaches creative writing and American Indian Studies classes at Haskell Indian Nations University. Her fifth collection of poems, *Thailand Journal,* is from Woodley Press (2003). She has won fellowships and other awards from the Lannan Foundation, National Endowment for the Humanities, Kansas Arts Council, Roberts Foundation, and Poetry Society of America (Pami Jurassi). Contact her at *deniselow9@hotmail.com.* ◯

Maya (Mary Hebert) lives in Brooklyn, New York. She is the author of *Horatio Rides the Wind* (Templar PLC) and contributing editor of *Not Black and White: Inside Words from the Bronx WritersCorps* (Plain View Press). Her poetry has appeared in several anthologies, including the 911 National Peace Poetry Project. She is currently compiling a text of sacred teachings, *Everyday a Feather Finds Me.* Contact her at *maryhebert@sprintmail.com.* ◯

Kathaleen McKay has enjoyed a lifelong love for the outdoors. Her favorite activities include photography, hiking, canoeing, reading, and writing. She has produced a variety of creative freelance work over the years. Kathaleen lives in Canada with her cherished daughter Caroline and their adorable canine pal Bill. Contact her at *kaymck@sprint.ca.* ◯

Karla Linn Merrifield teaches English composition at SUNY College at Brockport, New York, where she earned her M.A. in creative writing. Her poetry has been published in journals such as *Earth's Daughters, Negative Capability, Mediphors,* and *Boatman's Quarterly Review,* and in anthologies, including *Prairie Hearts: Women Write on the Midwest* and *To Honor Our Teachers.* When not teaching, she travels widely throughout the United States and Canada, writing poetry as she explores. Contact her at *kmerrifi@brockport.edu.* ◯

Philip Miller's poems have been published in *Poetry, Chelsea, Rattapallax,* and other journals. His most recent books are *Branches Snapping* (Helicon Nine Editions) and *Why We Love Our Cats and Dogs* (Unholy Day Press), a book of poems and short fiction co-authored with Patricia Lawson. Contact him at *riverfrontreadings@yahoo.com.* ◡

Warren Lane Molton is a pastoral counselor and couples therapist. He has served as a military chaplain in Korea, campus minister, professor of pastoral theology at two seminaries, and is the author of five books, including the popular *Friends, Partners and Lovers,* in print since 1979. He has published nearly 200 poems and articles in periodicals, with his most recent book, *If God Is,* available for review and purchase at *www.forestofpeace.com.* ◡

Mary Oberg is a registered nurse and energy healer. She is a graduate of Core Star Energy Healing and also completed an international certification in healing touch, endorsed by the American Holistic Nurses Association. She provides energy healing upon patient/family request and with a physician order at the medical center where she is employed. She also has a private practice in energy healing. Contact her at *healingtouch1@comcast.net.* ◡

Rev. Robert Pagliari, C.Ss.R., Ph.D., a Redemptorist priest living in New York City, has held several university teaching positions and was senior editor of religious publishing at Doubleday Press. He is associate director of Catholic Charities for the Archdiocese of New York. He holds four master's degrees (psychology, theology, education, and speech) and a Ph.D. in human communication. He authors a monthly column for the Catholic New York News Web site (*www.cny.org*) and can be contacted there. ◎

Liz Palika is a professional dog trainer in Vista, California. Her emphasis is on teaching both pets and therapy dogs. Liz is also a professional writer and has been published in *Newsweek*, the *Saturday Evening Post*, and all the major pet publications. Contact her at *www.lizpalika.com*. ◎

Colleen Palmer has worked for over twenty years in training and developing people, first as a psychotherapist, then as a business executive and consultant. She has a gift for being able to listen from the right side of the brain and has expanded this into a highly effective access for guiding people to remove repetitive obstacles. After living in Japan for five years, she now lives in Tucson, Arizona. Contact her at *cpalmer@spatial-dynamics.com*. ◎

Beverly Partridge, for the past ten years since her retirement from teaching, has been keeping a journal to find out what she believes. Her strong connection with the natural world stems from living and working on a Willamette Valley sheep farm for sixteen years. Since moving back to the city, she also pursues acrylic painting. Her poetry has been published in *Fireweed, Dakotah, Chadakoin Review,* and *From Here We Speak, An Anthology of Oregon Poetry.* ◎

Timothy Pettet was born in northern Idaho, 1948, and born again the first time he skipped a rock on Coeur d'Alene Lake. He moved twelve times by the time he was in the seventh grade. In Kansas City, he's as at home as he has ever been, touching water with the flat side of his fountain pen. ◌

Anne Ewing Rassios Ph.D., born in California of Texan roots, is a geoscientist who has lived and worked in Greece for the past three decades. Author of more than forty articles in geological and environmental sciences, her research has taken her throughout the lesser-known (including underground) terrains of Greece. Her first novel, *Godquake: Life on the Edge,* set in Greece, was published by Moose Hill Books in 2004. ◌

David Ray's books include *Demons in the Diner* (winner of the Richard J. Snyder Memorial Award), *The Tramp's Cup, Wool Highways* (winners of the William Carlos Williams Award), *The Maharani's New Wall, Kangaroo Paws,* and *Sam's Book* (recipient of the Maurice English Poetry Award). Other honors include the Nuclear Age Peace Foundation Poetry Award, the Allen Ginsberg Award, and a National Endowment for the Arts fellowship for fiction. His latest books are *One Thousand Years: Poems about the Holocaust* and *The Endless Search: A Memoir.* Contact him at *www.davidraypoet.com.* ◌

Judy Ray is coeditor with David Ray of *Fathers: A Collection of Poems* (St. Martin's Press). She is author of two books of poetry, *Pebble Rings* and *Pigeons in the Chandeliers,* and a prose memoir, *The Jaipur Sketchbook: Impressions of India.* Judy lives in Tucson, where she spends time as a volunteer teacher of English as a second language to adults in the community. Contact her at *www.davidraypoet.com.* ◌

Denise E. Richards is a sailor, traveler, photographer, chef, and amateur naturalist living in Portland, Oregon, with her husband Charles, and Zuma, their intrepid Labrador/husky companion. An award-winning public relations practitioner and adventuress, she is currently writing a book on the humorous and complex challenges of building and running her own inn and restaurant "off the grid" in the Costa Rican rain forest. Contact her at *lifescribe@comcast.net.* ◯

William Pitt Root's six books include *Trace Elements from a Recurring Kingdom* and *Faultdancing,* with more recent work in *Atlantic Monthly, Poetry, Commentary, Artful Dodge,* and *Rattapallax.* Translated into twenty languages, he's read recently in Sweden, Italy, Macedonia, and at the Bowery Poetry Club. He's held Guggenheim, Rockefeller, Stegner, and National Endowment for the Arts fellowships. Commuting weekly from his home near the Blue Ridge mountains, he teaches at Hunter College in Manhattan. ◯

Robert Rubinstein has authored *Curtains Up! Theatre Games & Storytelling; Hints For Teaching Success In Middle School* and two young adult novels, *Who Wants to Be a Hero!* and *When Sirens Scream.* He is a recipient of the National Storytelling Association's Oracle Award and has been featured in *NEA Today,* National Education Association's publication. Contact him at *www.thinkvideo.com/robertrubinstein.* ◯

Kim Runciman is a writer and editor in Seattle. She has published both fiction and nonfiction in a variety of publications, teaches copyediting, and recently served as editor of a monthly newspaper featuring natural foods, nutrition, health, and cooperatives. She may be contacted at *kimrunciman@yahoo.com*. ℘

Jeanne Ann Ryan is an energy healer, a reiki master, and a visionary artist. Jeanne is a graduate of Core Star Energy Healing, an instructor in Awakening Your Light Body coursework, and works with Symmetry rhythms and pulses. Her paintings are inspired by her inner sight. Contact her at *jaryan@midmo.com*. ℘

Mark G. Schroer is a lyricist and poet published in numerous poetry publications including *The Thorny Locust, The Same,* and the anthology *Show + Tell* (Potpourri Press, 2001), a collection of visual art and writing. As a lyricist, he has written for the bluegrass band The Smashing Bumpkins and for national jazz talent Angela Hagenbach. He spends his extra time as a residential contractor. Contact him at *markonly@hotmail.com*. ℘

Heather Sharfeddin lives in western Oregon with her husband and son. She spent her childhood in some of the most remote areas of Idaho and Montana and writes novels and short stories about life and the people of the West. She is also director of knowledge management for an international software company. Contact her at *hsharfeddin@yahoo.com*. ℘

Susan Kerr Shawn lives south of Portland, Oregon, with her husband Eric and their two beloved dogs. She is working on her first spiritual memoir, finding time to write between her work with clients and walking in nearby forests. She can be reached at *sshawn@teleport.com*. ℘

Contributors

Deborah Shouse is a writer, facilitator, and creativity catalyst. Deborah's personal stories have appeared in *Reader's Digest, Newsweek, Family Circle, Woman's Day, the Washington Post, and MS.* She has been featured in more than a dozen anthologies, including *Chicken Soup for the Worker's Soul.* Deborah is coauthor of *Making Your Message Memorable: Communicating Through Stories.* She loves stones and watches for them on every walk. Contact her at *www.thecreativityconnection.com.* ◎

Roberta Gordon Silver, also known as R. Gordon Silver, has master's degrees in counseling and special education. A member of Missouri Writers' Guild, her most recent publications include *Voices of Eternity,* an inspirational historical novel, and *Power Within,* a woman's adventure novel, both published by First Books Library. Contact her at *Silverbob765@yahoo.com.* ◎

Cris Staubach works as a children's librarian in New London and lives near Long Island Sound in Connecticut. She can't fathom wanting to live anywhere but on the coast of New England, with its rocky soil and pounding seas. Since childhood, she has communed with nature to connect her mind with a greater consciousness. Contact her at *castauba@portone.com.* ◎

Judith A. Stock delivers unique and insightful feature articles, service pieces, news, and essays to a diverse range of media including magazines, newspapers, corporate accounts, and Web sites. Her articles have appeared in *The Chicago Tribune, Smart Homeowner, Garden Compass, Dog Watch,* and *Catnip Newsletter.* She lives in Los Angeles. Contact her at *www.judithstock.com.* ◎

Tonweya shares her house with two cats, one bird, and many stones. She has written a children's book, *Earth Friends*, and says, "The music of my soul is singing as I travel down the road of life." Her adventures with stones are dedicated to A1 Bean "for truly being the wind beneath my wings and encouraging me to fly with the hawks." Contact her at *catwithwings1@aol.com*. ℘

Nancy Vorkink was born in New York, but her journeys have taken her far, including the remote villages of Africa, where she was a teacher. She considers herself a spiritual seeker. The circles of her journey often are rooted in her beloved Maine. She lives in Denver. Contact her at *n.vorkink@att.net*. ℘

Patricia Walkenhorst is a genealogist, researcher, and local historian, specializing in stories of the Irish settlers of Kansas. Her family history book, *The Callahans of Kansas*, has led her on a quest to understand the mystique of her Irish pioneer heritage. She lives in Blue Springs, Missouri. Contact her at *keepsake@sound.net*. ℘

Suella Walsh is author of several novels for children and numerous articles for adult fiction writers. She teaches writing classes and uses her book, *Creating Fiction That Sells: A Compilation of Published Magazine Articles*, as a class text. She is on the board of Whispering Prairie Press and is a prose editor for *Kansas City Voices Magazine*. Contact her at *landswalsh@prodigy.net*. ℘

Patricia Wellingham-Jones, former psychology researcher/writer/editor, has been published in journals, newspapers, and anthologies. She has won numerous awards and been the featured poet in several journals. Recent books are *Don't Turn Away: Poems About Breast Cancer; Labyrinth: Poems & Prose; Apple Blossoms at Eye Level,* and Lummox Press Little Red Book series, *A Gathering Glance.* She lives in northern California. Contact her at *www.snowcrest.net/pamelaj/wellingham jones/home.htm.* ☾

Valorie J. Wells, Ph.D., is a transplanted New Yorker who has returned to Kansas City "four times in ten years, so I guess this is my nest." Valorie is a certified clinical hypnotherapist and has a private practice within an integrative health care clinic. She is the proud mother of three daughters and has six grandchildren. Contact her at *drvjwells@planetkc.com.* ☾

Hannah Wilson's poetry and fiction have appeared in *Calyx, Prairie Schooner,* the *Portland Oregonian,* on Portland buses as part of *Poetry in Motion,* in baseball magazines, and in literary reviews. She has a poem in the *2004 Women Artists Datebook.* Supported by a grant from Literary Arts, she is working on a linked story collection about old women. Contact her at *hana@mindspring.com.* ☾

Jeanie Wilson's poetry and short stories have appeared in literary journals and anthologies. Her book, *Uncurling,* was published by Mid-America Press in 2000. Jeanie has presented her poems and short stories at numerous readings, including radio and television programs. Contact her at *jeaniewilson1@msn.com.* ☾

Thomas Zvi Wilson's book, *Deliberate and Accidental Acts*, (Thorpe Menn Award runner-up and Byron Caldwell Smith nominee), was published by BkMk Press. His poems have appeared widely in journals and anthologies. He has guest-lectured at seven universities, given numerous readings, edited considerable poetry, was Poet at Large sponsored by the National Endowment for the Arts, and was also panel judge for seven years for the Marianne Moore Poetry Award and John Ciardi Prize for Poetry. Contact him at *tzviwilson@msn.com.*

Judith Diana Winston is a visionary artist, photographer, and writer. Her book *Meditative Magic: The Pleiadean Glyphs,* a channeled work based on sacred geometry, is in its second printing. Her forthcoming book is *The Keeper Of The Diary.* Judith Diana sees her work as a marriage of her creativity with her spiritual journey. She lives in Santa Monica, California, is a hugger of trees, and a lover of all things wild. Contact her at *www.meditativemagic.com.*

Christopher Woods's recent books are *Under a Riverbed Sky,* prose poems and brief fictions from Panther Creek Press; and *Heart Speak,* stage monologues for actors from Stone River Press. Personal Space Theatrics in New York produced his play, *Moonbirds,* about census takers in an unpopulated desert country. Contact him at *dreamwood77019@hotmail.com.*

Contributors

Cherise Wyneken is retired from teaching and raising four children. She lives in Albany, California, and has enjoyed sharing her thoughts and experiences with readers through a variety of journals, periodicals, and anthologies, such as *Dorothy Parker's Elbow*, *Stories from Where We Live: California Coast*, and *Surviving Ophelia*. *Seeded Puffs*, her book of poetry, was published by Dry Bones Press, Inc. Contact her at *cwyneken@sbcglobal.net.*

To My Readers

If you have a comment, question, or story to share, I'd love to hear from you. Please contact me through my Web site at *www.sacredfeathers.com*.

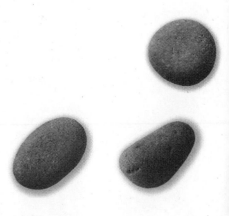